Multicolour Grammar Series
for Children

WREN

New Simple
English Grammar

4

Multicolour Grammar Series
for Children

WREN

New Simple
English Grammar

4

P.C. WREN
M.A. (OXON.), I.E.S

Revised By
N.D.V. PRASADA RAO
M.A., D.T.E., Ph.D.

S. CHAND
AN ISO 9001 : 2000 COMPANY

S. CHAND & COMPANY

RAM NAGAR, NEW DELHI - 110 055

Sole Distributors :

S. CHAND & COMPANY LTD.
(An ISO 9001 : 2000 Company)
Head Office : 7361, RAM NAGAR, NEW DELHI - 110 055
Phones : 23672080-81-82, 9899107446, 9911310888;
Fax : 91-11-23677446
Shop at: **schandgroup.com;** E-mail: **schand@vsnl.com**

Branches :

- 1st Floor, Heritage, Near Gujarat Vidhyapeeth, Ashram Road,
  Ahmedabad-380 014. Ph. 27541965, 27542369, ahmedabad@schandgroup.com
- No. 6, Ahuja Chambers, 1st Cross, Kumara Krupa Road,
  Bangalore-560 001. Ph : 22268048, 22354008, bangalore@schandgroup.com
- 238-A M.P. Nagar, Zone 1, **Bhopal** - 462 011. Ph : 4274723. bhopal@schandgroup.com
- 152, Anna Salai, **Chennai**-600 002. Ph : 28460026, chennai@schandgroup.com
- S.C.O. 2419-20, First Floor, **Sector- 2**2-C (Near Aroma Hotel), Chandigarh-160022,
  Ph-2725443, 2725446, chandigarh@schandgroup.com
- 1st Floor, Bhartia Tower, Badambadi, **Cuttack**-753 009, Ph-2332580; 2332581,
  cuttack@schandgroup.com
- 1st Floor, 52-A, Rajpur Road, **Dehradun**-248 001. Ph : 2740889, 2740861,
  dehradun@schandgroup.com
- Pan Bazar, **Guwahati**-781 001. Ph : 2514155, guwahati@schandgroup.com
- Sultan Bazar, **Hyderabad**-500 195. Ph : 24651135, 24744815, hyderabad@schandgroup.com
- Mai Hiran Gate, **Jalandhar** - 144008 . Ph. 2401630, 5000630, jalandhar@schandgroup.com
- A-14 Janta Store Shopping Complex, University Marg, Bapu Nagar, **Jaipur** - 302 015,
  Phone : 2719126, jaipur@schandgroup.com
- 613-7, M.G. Road, Ernakulam, **Kochi**-682 035. Ph : 2381740, cochin@schandgroup.com
- 285/J, Bipin Bihari Ganguli Street, **Kolkata**-700 012. Ph : 22367459, 22373914,
  kolkata@schandgroup.com
- Mahabeer Market, 25 Gwynne Road, Aminabad, **Lucknow**-226 018. Ph : 2626801, 2284815,
  lucknow@schandgroup.com
- Blackie House, 103/5, Walchand Hirachand Marg , Opp. G.P.O., **Mumbai**-400 001.
  Ph : 22690881, 22610885, mumbai@schandgroup.com
- Karnal Bag, Model Mill Chowk, Umrer Road, **Nagpur**-440 032 Ph : 2723901, 2777666
  nagpur@schandgroup.com
- 104, Citicentre Ashok, Govind Mitra Road, **Patna**-800 004. Ph : 2300489, 2302100,
  patna@schandgroup.com

By an arrangement with
MANECKJI COOPER EDUCATION TRUST
Mumbai

ISBN : 81-219-2333-6
Code : 11 814
PRINTED IN INDIA
*By Rajendra Ravindra Printers (Pvt.) Ltd., 7361, Ram Nagar, New Delhi-110 055
and published by S. Chand & Company. 7361,
Ram Nagar, New Delhi-110 055*

PREFACE

P.C. Wren's **New English Grammar Series,** comprising six books, can be classed among the best and most authoritative of traditional grammars for children. These graded books contain a systematic treatment of English grammatical forms and lead up to P.C. Wren and H. Martin's monumental work **High School English Grammar and Composition.**

The aim of the revision of the present series is to make the books more suitable for use in the modern classroom. Apart from the learner-friendly format and attractive illustrations, the features of these new editions are as follows :

1. Some grammar rules and structures have been revised or recast so as to bring them into line with current usage. For example, the use of **me, him, us,** etc. after **than** and **as** in comparisons and the use of **who** as the object of a verb or preposition, which were frowned upon in P.C. Wren's time, are now considered correct. Sentences like "He is taller than **me"**, **"Who** do you want?" and " **Who** are you talking about?" are correct.

2. Some chapters have been expanded or recast so as to reflect the new developments in the study of English structure and usage. The chapters dealing with tenses and modals have been completely rewritten.

3. The material dealing with analysis has been considerably cut down.

4. A number of sentences, outdated in content, have been replaced with new ones, mainly relating to modern times.

5. A lot of activity-based material has been added. Some of the exercises include pair-work and group-work activities.

It is hoped that the above-mentioned aspects of the revision, which largely reflect the present-day trends in pedagogic grammar, will increase the usefulness of these books and add to their popularity.

The contribution made by Dr (Mrs) Shalini Verma, Editor, School Books, and the Editorial Team of Messrs S. Chand & Company to the final shape of this book needs special mention.

N.D.V. PRASADA RAO

NOTE TO THE TEACHER

The fourth book of the **Grammar Series for Children,** written by P.C. Wren, includes a comprehensive grammar syllabus, incorporating systematic work on listening, speaking, reading, writing and activity oriented exercises. It takes an integrated approach to young learner's training and revision. The book has unique double folded features, namely:

(i) task based element.

(ii) 'discovery' approach to the teaching of grammar basics.

Our grammar syllabus includes work on different **parts of speech, kinds of nouns, case of nouns, pronouns, verbs, adjectives & adverbs and their degrees of comparison, articles, kinds of sentences, tenses '–ing form' & to–infinitive, active & passive voice, mood, subject-verb agreement, enlargement of the subject & the object, extension of the predicate and analysis of simple sentences.** It aims to provide thorough coverage and practice exercises well suited for the young learners through :

* Rich illustrations to help children perceive faster.

* Examples synergic with illustrations.

* Added information/teaching technique given in form of "Note to the teacher".

* Short definitions given in highlighted boxes.

* Ample number of exercises to support the 'learning by doing' method.

CONTENTS

Chapter 1

The Sentence

When we speak or write, we use words.

We use these words in groups.

When a group of words makes *complete sense*, we call it a **Sentence;** as,

Mary had a little lamb.

Little Jack Horner sat in a corner.

The girl is reading.

Look at my kite.

Why are you standing here ?

A **Sentence** *is a group of words which makes complete sense.*

EXERCISE 1

Which of the following groups of words are *Sentences* ?

1. My friend Rama.
2. The wind is cold.
3. Barking dogs.
4. She is a good girl.
5. Behind the door.
6. Birds fly.
7. The express bus.
8. On the desk.

9. Fire burns.
10. My sister and my brother.
11. In the fridge.
12. The phone rang.
13. That new computer.
14. On Channel 12.
15. Switch it off.

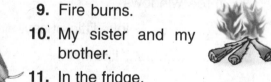

SUBJECT AND PREDICATE

Every sentence that we speak or write consists of two parts.

1. We must talk about some *person* or *thing*, if we talk at all.
2. We must *say* something about that person or thing.

In other words, we must have a *subject* to talk about and we must *say* or *predicate* something about that subject.

If I come up to you and say "Your father," you know that that is the subject about which I wish to talk. But I have said nothing about that subject. To make a sentence I must say something about your father.

If I say "Your father knows me," I have expressed a *complete* thought. I have made a sentence.

EXERCISE 2

A. Say something about the following *Subjects* :

Rama, cows, Mumbai, birds, the sun, the television, Mahatma Gandhi.

B. Group work

Read your sentences to each other in groups of five and discuss which sentences are correct or the best.

EXERCISE 3

The following groups of words are not sentences. They do not express complete thoughts. They have no subjects. Give each one a *Subject*.

1. .... is sweet.

2. .... caught a mouse.

3. .... has three windows.

4. .... love little pussy.

5. .... like milk.

6. .... build nests.

7. .... is crowing.

8. How well .... sings !

9. .... is ringing.

10. Once upon a time there lived ....

In grammar, *that about which something is said* is called the **Subject**. *What is said about the subject* is called the **Predicate**.

Notice how the following sentences are divided into Subject and Predicate :

Subject	Predicate
Birds	fly.
Cows	eat grass.
Mary	had a little lamb.
The horse	is white.
Old Mother Hubbard	went to the cupboard.

Divide each of the following sentences into *Subject* and *Predicate*:

1. Mary had a little lamb.

2. Simple Simon met a pieman.

3. Humpty Dumpty sat on a wall.

4. Little Bo-Peep lost her sheep.

5. Birds build nests in trees.

6. He goes to church on Sundays.

7. The village master taught his little school.

8. A barking sound the shepherd hears.

9. Into the street the Piper stepped.

10. My new watch keeps good time.

11. Under a spreading chestnut-tree the village smithy stands.

A sentence may consist of a single word, like "Run!" or "Answer". Where this is the case, it is clear that one part of the sentence has not been expressed, although it has been understood. This part is the Subject.

If I shout "Run" to you, I mean "You run."

If you knock at my door, and I say "Come in," you understand that I mean "You come in," although I omit the Subject of my sentence.

Chapter 2

The Noun

Name of a person, animal, place or thing.

Read these sentences :

1. **Saroja** has been to the **market**.
2. Where is the **dog** ?
3. There is a **book** on the **desk**.

The words in *bold* are naming words. **Saroja** is the name of a person. **Market** is the name of a place. **Dog** is the name of an animal. **Book** and **desk** are the names of things. Words like these are called *Nouns*.

A *Noun* is the name of a person, animal, place or thing.

EXERCISE 1

Pick out the *Nouns* in the following sentences :

1. The cow gives milk.
2. Mice fear cats.
3. Ants are always busy.
4. Ashoka was a great king.
5. My books are in my desk.
6. The sun is in the sky.
7. Bread is made from flour.
8. The earth goes round the sun.
9. The dog ran after the thief.
10. Birds build nests in trees.

11. The wolf killed the goat.
12. I see a bird on that tree.
13. I have a green parrot.
14. Is there any water in that pot ?
15. Foxes live in holes in the ground.
16. Rabbits have short tails.

17. Hari wrote a letter to his father.
18. The bullock is in the field.

19. There are two chairs in this room.

20. This room has two doors and five windows.

21. There are three boys on that bench.

22. Mahatma Gandhi is called the Father of the Nation.

23. We have put all our records on computer.

24. Albert Einstein was born in Germany.

25. Mother has bought some grapes.

EXERCISE 2

Write down ten *Nouns*.

1. ....
2. ....
3. ....
4. ....
5. ....
6. ....
7. ....
8. ....
9. ....
10. ....

Chapter 3

Kinds of Nouns

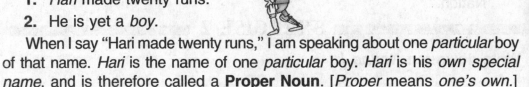

Read these sentences :

1. *Hari* made twenty runs.
2. He is yet a *boy*.

When I say "Hari made twenty runs," I am speaking about one *particular* boy of that name. *Hari* is the name of one *particular* boy. *Hari* is his *own special name*, and is therefore called a **Proper Noun**. [*Proper* means *one's own*.]

> A *Proper Noun* is the special name of a particular person or place; as, Abdul, Rama, Sita, Shirin, Mumbai, Kolkata, London.

Note: A Proper Noun always begins with a capital letter.

The name *boy* may be given to any and every boy — to Hari, Rama, Abdul, Sohrab, Jack, etc. It does not belong specially to any one particular boy. It is a name *common* to all boys. It is, therefore, called a **Common Noun.**

> A *Common Noun* is a name given in common to every person or thing of the same class or kind; as,

> man, woman, boy, girl, cow, horse, town, country, book, desk.

Note again :

Shirin is a Proper Noun, while *girl* is a Common Noun.

Rama is a Proper Noun, while *boy* is a Common Noun.

Chennai is a Proper Noun, while *city* is a Common Noun.

India is a Proper Noun, while *country* is a Common Noun.

A Proper Noun sometimes consists of several words, *e.g.*, such a name as *Mother Teresa Girls' High School*. It is the name of only one school, though it consists of five words.

EXERCISE 1

Pick out the *Proper Nouns* in the following sentences :

1. Abdul and Latif are brothers.

2. Mr Lal is flying to Singapore on Friday.
3. Delhi is the capital of India.

New Simple English Grammar

4. Aladdin had a wonderful lamp.
5. Mary had a little lamb.
6. Nelson is famous for his victory at Trafalgar.
7. My cousin has a dog called Fido.

================ **EXERCISE 2** ================

Make four sentences, each containing a *Proper Noun*.

....

....

....

....

Read the sentence :

The boy showed great *courage.*

We can see the *sun;* we can touch a *book;* but can we see or touch *courage* ? No; it is the name of something that we can only think of. Such a name is called an **Abstract Noun.**

An **Abstract Noun** *is the name of something that we can only think of;* as,
sweetness, weakness, pity, hope, doubt, greed, childhood, misery, honesty, sleep, death.

================ **EXERCISE 3** ================

Pick out the *Abstract Nouns* in the following sentences :

1. He lost his parents in infancy.
2. Health is wealth.
3. The elephant has great strength.
4. They groped their way in darkness.
5. The wall is twenty centimetres in thickness.
6. Warmth is necessary to life.
7. Rama's words filled Sita's heart with gladness.
8. The streets of this town are noted for their crookedness.
9. Without health there is no happiness.
10. Never tell a lie.
11. Wisdom is better than strength.
12. I often think of the happy days of childhood.

Make three sentences, each containing an *Abstract Nouns*.

....

....

....

When a noun is the name of a number (or *collection*) of persons or things considered as one, such as, *class, army, crowd, flock,* it is called a **Collective Noun.**

The word *flock* is a Collective Noun, because it is the name given to a *collection* of sheep or goats.

The word *crowd* is a Collective Noun, because it is the name given to a *collection* of people.

A **Collective Noun** *is the name of a number of people or things considered as one; as, flock, crowd, team army.*

Pick out the *Nouns* in the following sentences and say whether they are *Common, Proper, Abstract,* or *Collective* :

1. A cold wind blew last night.
2. The girl has a sweet voice.
3. The people who live in Holland are called Dutch.
4. There was a large crowd in the street.
5. The child has caught a cold.
6. Are you speaking the truth ?
7. Columbus discovered America.
8. Mumbai is a big city.
9. A florist sells flowers.
10. Solomon was famous for his wisdom.
11. He treats his children with great kindness.
12. Agra has many fine buildings.
13. Ashoka was a great king.
14. The wind and the sun had a quarrel.
15. We watched the match with interest.
16. Kolkata is on the banks of the Hooghli.
17. The girl showed great courage.
18. Sohrab gave his sister a great fright.
19. Our class consists of twenty pupils.
20. Honesty is the best policy.

Another classification of nouns is whether they are "countable" or "uncountable".

Countable Nouns (or Countables) are the names of things which we can count, *e.g.*, book, pen, computer, apple, flower. We say "one book", "two books", "five books", etc. Countable nouns can be singular or plural.

Uncountable Nouns (or Uncountables) are the names of things which we cannot count, *e.g.*, milk, rice, petrol, electricity, gold, honesty, friendship. We cannot say "one milk", "two milks", "five milks", and so on. Uncountable nouns do not have plural forms. Abstract nouns and names of substances are uncountable in most cases.

EXERCISE 6

Say which of the following nouns are *Countable* and which *Uncountable*:

1. chair	2. house	3. water
4. cup	5. wheat	6. music
7. song	8. cleverness	9. cotton
10. film	11. happiness	12. telephone
13. honey	14. jar	15. silver

EXERCISE 7

Put *Nouns* in the blank spaces :

1. .... crow in the morning.

2. .... should obey their parents.

3. .... build nests in trees.

4. Many .... grow in my garden.

5. The .... shows us the time.

6. I ran fast, but I missed the ....

7. The .... rises in the east.

8. A cold .... blew last night.

9. Rain comes from the ....

10. Is there any .... in that pot ?

11. The cow gives us ....

12. We see with our ....

13. The .... sat on the branch and cawed.

14. Monkeys have long ....

15. We must eat our .... slowly.

16. The .... barked loudly.

17. We hear with our ....

18. Woollen .... are best in cold weather.

Read the sentences below. The words in italic type are *Verbs*.

Miss Jones *teaches* English.

Gopal *kicked* the ball.

The glass *broke*.

What does Miss Jones do ? She *teaches* ......

What did Gopal do ? He *kicked* .....

What happened to the glass ? It *broke*.

A ***Verb*** says what somebody or something does or what happens.

Words like *be* (= *am, is, was,* etc), *remain,seem* are also called verbs. They express a state, as in the following sentences :

The movie "Titanic" *was* a big hit.

They *remained* silent.

Radha *seems* tired.

A ***Verb*** is a word which expresses an action, event or state.

The word "verb" means "word". It is so called because it is *the* word (meaning, the most important word) in a sentence. *You cannot make a sentence without a verb.* A sentence may contain only one word, but that word must be a verb.

Note that a verb is not always one word. It often consists of more than one word; as,

Sita *is singing*.

He *was kicked* by a horse.

She *will come* tomorrow.

The book *has been found*.

EXERCISE 1

Pick out the *Verbs* in the following sentences :

1. The girl sings sweetly.
2. The boy stood on the burning deck.
3. Cocks crow in the morn.
4. Cats see in the dark.
5. The boy fell in the water.
6. I met a little cottage girl.
7. Children like mangoes.
8. Little Jack Horner sat in a corner.
9. The picture hangs on the wall.
10. The king rode on a white horse.

EXERCISE 2

Put *Verbs* in the blank spaces :

1. Birds .... nests in trees.
2. The tailor .... me a new coat.
3. The snake .... the man.
4. We .... cricket.
5. All the boys .... their teacher.
6. The gang of robbers .... in a cave.
7. Two and two .... four.  2 + 2 = 4
8. The headmaster .... him his name.
9. The dog .... at the man.
10. Birds .... with their wings.

EXERCISE 3

Write down ten sentences and underline the *Verb* in each.

....
....
....
....
....

5

Kinds of Verbs

Read these sentences :

1. The boy *made* a kite.

2. The boy *laughed.*

If I say to you "The boy made," I do not make complete sense. You want to know *what* the boy made.

When I say "The boy made a kite." I name the object which he made. The word *kite* is therefore called the **Object** of the verb *made.*

> The verb *made,* which requires an Object to complete its sense, is called a **Transitive Verb.**

If I say "The boy laughed," I make complete sense. You know what the boy did. He *laughed.* The verb by itself makes good sense.

> Such a verb as the verb *laughed* that does not require an Object, but makes good sense by itself, is called an **Intransitive Verb**.

It will be seen that Transitive Verbs require an Object to complete the sense; Intransitive Verbs do not require any Object to complete the sense.

Transitive Verbs	**Intransitive Verbs**
Hari *shut* the window.	The child still *lives.*
Karim *opened* the door.	Some animals *swim.*
Rama *saw* a snake.	The poor woman *wept.*

EXERCISE 1

Pick out the *Verbs* in the following sentences, and tell in each case whether the verb is *Transitive* or *Intransitive*. Where the verb is Transitive, name the *Object* :

1. Bad boys hide their faults.

2. Some boys threw stones at the frogs.

3. The fire burnt the house.

4. The sun rises in the east.

5. The frog jumped out of the pond.

6. The goat fell into the well.

7. I know a funny little man.

New Simple English Grammar

8. Humpty Dumpty sat on a wall.

9. Go and see your father tomorrow.

10. Take your books and go home.

EXERCISE 2

A. Complete the following by supplying an *Object* :

1. The horse kicked ....

2. The teacher punished ....

3. Hari worked .... correctly.

4. My brother wrote this ....

5. He broke ....

6. The cow gives ....

7. The sun gives ....

8. The mason built ....

9. The tailor made ....

10. The policeman caught ....

B. Group work

Read your answers to each other in groups of five. Discuss the differences in your answers and decide which are correct or the best.

There are only a few verbs which are always Intransitive. Most verbs can be used either Transitively or Intransitively.

Used Transitively	*Used Intransitively*
Many people *eat* rice.	Wise people *eat* slowly.
He *wrote* novels.	He *writes* legibly.
The driver *stopped* the train.	The train *stopped* suddenly.
His teacher *speaks* several languages.	The child *speaks* plainly.
He *breathed* a prayer for help.	The dying man scarcely *breathed*.
He *walked* his horse up and down.	He *walked* up and down.

Before you say whether a Verb is Transitive or Intransitive carefully examine *how it is used.*

EXERCISE 3

Write down five sentences, each containing a verb used *Intransitively*.

EXERCISE 4

Write down five sentences, each containing a verb used *Transitively*.

Chapter 6

The Adjective

Read these sentences :

1. Rama is a *smart* boy.
2. *Lazy* students fail.
3. Govind is *poor* but *honest*.
4. America is a *rich* country.

The above sentences contain a number of nouns which you can easily pick out. With some of these nouns there is a *describing-word*. By the help of these describing-words, we know something more about the person or thing named by each noun.

Thus, the word *smart* tells *what kind* of boy Rama is.

The word *lazy* tells *what kind* of students fail.

The words *poor* and *honest* tell *what kind* of man Govind is.

The word *rich* tells *what kind* of country America is.

In grammar, describing-words are called **Adjectives**. They are so called because they *add something to the meaning of a noun.*

[*Adjective* means *added to.*]

EXERCISE 1

Pick out the *Adjectives* in the following sentences, and say why you think they are adjectives :

1. The horse is a noble animal.
2. Kolkata is a big city.
3. Lead is a heavy metal.
4. The cow is a useful animal.
5. The rose is a beautiful flower.
6. Ahmed is a poor man.
7. Our school has a large playground.
8. Dhondu is a cruel fellow.
9. Radha is a sweet singer.
10. Mumbai has a fine harbour.
11. Mary has a little lamb.
12. Mr Pai is a rich merchant.

Mr. Pai

13. Akbar was a wise king.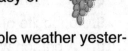

14. Noshirwan was a just ruler.

15. This is a useful book.

16. Varanasi is a holy city.

17. Monkeys have long tails.

18. Aladdin had a wonderful lamp.

19. The world is a happy place.

20. The grapes are sour.

21. The food is delicious.

22. Is the sum easy or hard ?

23. We had terrible weather yesterday.

24. This is the oldest temple in the city.

EXERCISE 2

Can you solve this crossword ? The words are all *Adjectives*.

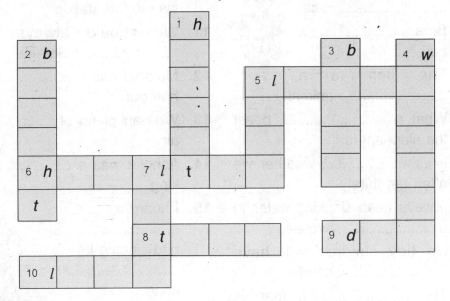

CLUES

Down

1. An ...... person is one who always tells the truth and never steals or cheats.

2. opposite of "dull"

3. opposite of "timid"

4. A person who has a lot of money

5. If you are .... , you will fail the exam.

7. opposite of "early"

Across

5. opposite of "small"

6. If you stop smoking, you will be ....

8. A ...... friend is one who helps you when you really need help.

9. opposite of "wet"

10. A person who is not able to walk well because of injury to the legs or feet.

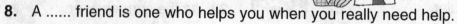

EXERCISE 3

Put *Adjectives* in the blank spaces :

1. The girl has a .... voice.

2. Be a .... boy.

3. The lion is a .... animal.

4. What a .... beast the elephant is !

5. In .... weather we often get thirsty.

6. Always keep drinking water in a ....vessel.

7. No tidy children will have .... hands.

8. The .... man is walking with a crutch.

9. Ah ! What a .... mistake I made !

10. Which is the .... way to the station ?

11. We should always wear ....clothes.

12. Mumbai has a .... harbour.

13. We want plenty of .... air.

14. Ashoka was a .... king.

15. I heard a .... bird singing its .... song.

16. A giraffe has a .... neck.

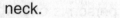

Chapter 7 — Kinds of Adjectives

Read these sentences :

1. Hamid was a *great* soldier.
2. Mumbai is a *big* city.

The word *great* is an Adjective which tells *what kind* of soldier Hamid was.

The word *big* is an Adjective which tells *what kind* of city Mumbai is.

> Such adjectives, which tell us of *what kind* a person or thing is, are called **Adjective of Quality**. Because they *describe* a person or thing, they are also called **Descriptive Adjectives**.

Adjectives of Quality answer the question "Of what kind ?"

EXERCISE 1

Pick out the *Adjectives of Quality* in the following sentences :

1. I know a funny little man.
2. His hair is crisp, and black, and long.
3. King Francis was a hearty king, and loved a royal sport.
4. Rahul Dravid is a brilliant batsman.
5. A barking sound the shepherd hears.
6. The way was long, the wind was cold, the stage performer was infirm and old.
7. There were bad mistakes in the exercise, and it was written on dirty, grey paper with thin, cheap ink.
8. I like the little pedlar who has a crooked nose.

EXERCISE 2

Write down three sentences, each containing two *Adjectives of Quality*.

....
....
....

Read these sentences :

1. *Four* boys ran down the street.
2. There are *twenty* boys in this class.
3. He has *much* money.
4. There is *little* hope of victory.
5. Shakespeare wrote *many* plays.
6. I want *some* money.

Some adjectives do not describe persons or things; they tell their *number* or *amount.*

Thus in the above six sentences each noun has an adjective which does not tell us *what kind* — but *how many* or *how much.*

Such adjectives, which tell us *how many* or *how much,* are called **Adjectives of Quantity.**

Adjectives of Quantity answer the question "How many?" or "How much ?"

EXERCISE 3

Pick out the *Adjectives of Quantity* in the following sentences:

1. Step back three paces.
2. I have told you this many times already.
3. I speak these few words to all men.
4. He is ninety years of age.
5. I bought some bananas.

6. Did you get many marks ?
7. Mary has six books in her bag.
8. He made five goals during the third match of the season, in spite of little training and some illness.

EXERCISE 4

Write down three sentences, each containing an *Adjective of Quantity*.

....

....

....

Read these sentences :

1. Come and look at *this* snake.
2. Look at *that* tree.
3. I like *these* bananas.
4. What is *that* girl writing?
5. I want *those* mangoes, not the others.
6. I hate *such* things.

It is clear that the adjectives in the above sentences are used, like a pointing finger to *point out* the thing or person that is spoken about.

Such *pointing-out* adjectives are called **Demonstrative Adjectives.**

They answer the question "which?"

EXERCISE 5

Pick out the *Demonstrative Adjectives* in the following sentences:

1. I don't like those friends of yours.

2. On yonder hills my father feeds his flock.

3. Do you think these boots would fit you ?

4. Is this book the one you want ?

5. Oh ! Do look at that funny kitten.

6. Would you like these bananas?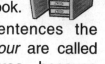

EXERCISE 6

Write down three sentences, each containing a *Demonstrative Adjective*.

Read these sentences :

1. *What* manner of man is he ?

2. *Which* way shall we go ?

3. *Which* banana do you want ?

In the above sentences the adjectives *what* and *which* ask questions. They are therefore called **Interrogative Adjectives**.

Read these sentences :

1. This is *my* desk.

2. That is *your* book.

In the above sentences the adjectives *my* and *your* are called **Possessive Adjectives**, because they tell *whose* a thing is.

EXERCISE 7

Pick out the *Adjectives* in the following sentences, and say what kind of adjective each one is, and what noun it belongs to :

1. The poor old woman gets little food.

2. I saw several sheep in that valley.

3. This mango is ripe.

4. One little lamb was lame.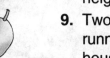

5. I want some money.

6. That idle fellow, Abdul, is the nineteenth boy in the class.

7. There is little water in the tank.

8. That cat belongs to my neighbours.

9. Two boys came running from the house.

10. That poor man has few friends.

11. He wastes less time and takes more trouble.

12. Three feet make one yard.

13. Akbar reigned for forty-nine years.

14. The spider has eight legs.

15. Shirin and Parvati are close friends.

16. One lovely hand she stretched for aid.

17. My favourite game is cricket.

18. Look at that lazy foolish fellow !

19. A straight and wide road runs to the barracks.

20. Happy and prosperous days await him.

EXERCISE 8

Put *Adjectives* in the blank spaces :

1. A week has .... days.

2. Does your watch keep .... time ?

3. Subhash Chandra Bose was a .... patriot.

4. The elephant is a .... animal.

5. .... tigers are man-eaters.

6. The hand has .... fingers.

7. This book cost me .... rupees.

8. The days are hot, but the nights are ....

9. Quinine is bitter, but honey is ....

10. Ice is cold, but steam is ....

11. Is this .... book ?

12. .... pen do you want ?

13. .... mangoes are ripe ?

14. .... book is this ?

15. .... fridge is better than .... fridge.

Chapter 8 — The Adverb

Read these sentences :

1. The king replied *angrily*.
2. Rama goes to school *daily*.
3. The child looked *up*.

In sentence 1 the word *angrily* is added to the verb *replied* to tell *how* the king replied.

In sentence 2 the word *daily* is added to the verb *goes* to tell *when* Rama goes to school.

In sentence 3 the word *up* is added to the verb *looked* to tell *where* the child looked.

Each of these words which *adds* something to the meaning of a *verb* is called an **Adverb**.

EXERCISE 1

Pick out the *Adverbs* in the following sentences, and name the verb with which each is used :

1. The sun shines brightly.
2. We must eat our food slowly.
3. The woman spoke loudly.
4. You have done your lesson well.
5. The soldiers fought fiercely.
6. The horse galloped fast.
7. The play will begin now.
8. My uncle lives here.
9. Gopal is standing there.
10. We should always speak the truth.

EXERCISE 2

Write down three sentences, each containing an *Adverb*.

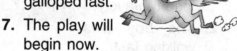

....

....

....

New Simple English Grammar

21

9   Kinds of Adverbs

Read these sentences :

1. He writes *badly*.
2. He spends his money *foolishly*.
3. He hit the ball *hard*.

What do you notice about the adverbs in these sentences ? They all show *how* the action is done.

How does he write ? .... Badly.

How does he spend his money ? .... Foolishly.

How did he hit the ball ? .... Hard.

These adverbs, which show the *manner* in which some action is done, are called **Adverbs of Manner**.

Adverbs of Manner answer the question "How ?"

EXERCISE 1

Pick out the *Adverbs of Manner* in the following sentences, and name the verb with which each is used.

1. The soldiers fought bravely.
2. The boy was walking fast.
3. They were talking loudly.
4. You should not do so.
5. She writes well.

6. He could not speak distinctly.
7. He loved her truly.
8. He spoke quietly.
9. The dog barked loudly.
   ba ba...
10. We were received kindly.

EXERCISE 2

Write down three sentences, each containing an *Adverb of Manner*.

....

....

....

Read these sentences :

1. The train stops *here*.
2. We live *there*.
3. My father has gone *out*.
4. The rocket went *up*.

Each of the adverbs in the above sentences shows *where* the action is done; *e.g.,*

Where does the train stop ? .... Here.

These adverbs, which show *where* some action is done, are called **Adverbs of Place**.

Adverbs of Place answer the question "Where ?"

EXERCISE 3

Pick out the *Adverbs of Place* in the following sentences :

1. He has come back.
2. The little lamb followed Mary everywhere.
3. Let us go out.
4. The servant has gone upstairs.
5. The peon is standing outside.
6. We sat inside.
7. Come in and sit down.
8. Work hard or you'll be kept in.

EXERCISE 4

Write down three sentences, each containing an *Adverb of Place*.

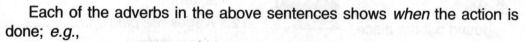

....

....

....

Read these sentences :

1. The holidays will begin *tomorrow*.
2. Work all the harder *today*.
3. I shall return *soon*.
4. Rama wrote to me *yesterday*.
5. Do it *now*.

Each of the adverbs in the above sentences shows *when* the action is done; *e.g.,*

When will the holidays begin ? .... Tomorrow.

These Adverbs, which show *when* some action is done, are called **Adverbs of Time.**

Adverbs of Time answer the question "When ?"

EXERCISE 5

Pick out the *Adverbs of Time* in the following sentences :

1. You may go now.
2. The end soon came.
3. I hurt my knee yesterday.
4. Wasted time never returns.
5. He is going to Chennai shortly.
6. I shall come afterwards.
7. Lately he has become lazy.
8. Once I heard the cuckoo sing.
9. I shall get a letter tomorrow.
10. Today I got up early.
11. Formerly we lived in Kolkata.
12. That day he arrived late.
13. Never speak rudely to anyone.
14. Obey me instantly.
15. My father comes here daily, but my brother seldom comes.
16. Sometimes I think he'll never get well.

EXERCISE 6

Write down three sentences, each containing an *Adverb of Time*.

....

....

....

EXERCISE 7

Fill up the blanks with suitable *Adverbs* :

1. The child is .... hurt.
2. The rain came on ....
3. He writes ....
4. He waited .... at the station.
5. We .... found out the place.
6. The exercise is .... written.
7. We ....live in our old house.
8. He ....comes to see us now.
9. Did you see Hari ....?
10. The gardener waters the plants ....
11. .... four boys are absent.
12. Wages are paid .... in our factory.
13. I looked for my pen-knife ....
14. That old man walks ....
15. These men work ....
16. The fire burns ....

Chapter 10

Kinds of Adverbs
(Contd.)

WORDS USED WITH ADJECTIVES TO ADD SOMETHING TO THEIR MEANING	Very beautiful
	Almost ripe
	Nearly full

Read these sentences :

1. The rose is *very* beautiful.
2. His face was *nearly* black.
3. The man was *almost* angry.

The word *very* is used with the Adjective *beautiful*, and tells **how** (or *to what degree*) *beautiful* the rose is.

The word *nearly* is used with the Adjective *black,* and tells **how** *black* his face was.

The word *almost* is used with the Adjective *angry*, and tells **how** *angry* the man was.

The words *very, nearly* and *almost,* which are thus used with Adjectives to add something to their meaning, are called **Adverbs of Degree**.

EXERCISE 1

Pick out the *Adverbs of Degree* in the following sentences:

1. He is very kind to his servant.
2. These mangoes are almost ripe.
3. You are quite wrong.
4. The cup is nearly full.
5. We spent a very pleasant day.
6. He is somewhat lazy.
7. This sum is quite easy.
8. He is too shy.
9. She is rather busy.
10. I am so glad to hear it.

Write down three sentences each containing an *Adverb of Degree*.

....

....

....

Read these sentences :

1. The boy runs *very* quickly.
2. He speaks *rather* slowly.

3. She drove *most* carefully.

The word *very* is used with the Adverb *quickly,* and tells **how** *quickly* the boy runs.

The word *rather* is used with the Adverb *slowly,* and tells **how** *slowly* he speaks.

The word *most* is used with the Adverb *carefully,* and tells **how** carefully she drove.

The words *very, rather* and *most,* which are thus used with Adverbs to add something to their meaning, are also called **Adverbs of Degree.**

It will be noticed that, unlike other Adverbs, an Adverb of Degree adds something to the meaning of an Adjective or another Adverb.

We may now say that *an **Adverb** is a word used with a verb, or an adjective, or another adverb to add something to its meaning.*

EXERCISE 3

Pick out the *Adverbs of Degree* in the following sentences:

1. He spoke very kindly to them.

2. The day passed very pleasantly.

3. He writes extremely well.

4. Please work less noisily.

5. He writes quite beautifully.

6. The newspapers wrote fairly accurately about the matter.

7. I do not want to see visitors too often today.

8. We missed you so much.

9. He works remarkably well.

10. I like Rama because he works so honestly and straightforwardly.

EXERCISE 4

Fill up the blanks with suitable *Adverbs of Degree* :

1. She sings .... well.
2. The sea was .... stormy.
3. He is .... careless.
4. You are .... right.
5. We got up .... early.
6. I am .... glad to hear it.
7. Are you .... sure ?
8. He is now .... better.
9. The distance was .... long.
10. We were .... kindly received.

Read these sentences :

1. *When* did you come?
2. *Where* is Abdul ?
3. *How* did you do it ?
4. *Why* are you late ?

In the above sentences the words *when, where, how, why* are adverbs which are used in *asking questions.* They are therefore called **Interrogative Adverbs.**

EXERCISE 5

Pick out the *Adverbs* in the following sentences, state their kinds and name the words they modify :

1. Slowly and sadly we laid him down.
2. Things are not better at present.
3. The weather is delightfully cool.
4. He is old enough to know better.
5. How brightly the moon shines !
6. How did you manage it ?
7. I shall be there presently.
8. He went quickly from the house but soon returned there.

EXERCISE 6

Fill up the blanks with suitable *Adverbs* :

1. I hurt my knee ....
2. You have not worked the sum ....
3. It is a good thing to go to bed ....
4. We must eat our food ....

5. An elephant will .... walk into deep soft mud.
6. The little lamb followed Mary ....
7. ....obey your teacher.

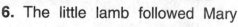

11

The Pronoun

Listen to Rama; *he* is singing. Govind and Ganpat are here. *They* have come to hear *him*. *He* will be glad to see *them*.

In the above sentences the words in italics are used *instead of* names (or nouns). It is easier and better to use such words than to keep on repeating the nouns and say—

Listen to Rama; Rama is singing. Govind and Ganpat are here. Govind and Ganpat have come to hear Rama. Rama will be glad to see Govind and Ganpat.

Such words, which are used *for* or *instead of nouns*, are called **Pronouns**.

The word Pronoun means "*for* a noun".

*A **Pronoun** is a word which is used instead of a noun.*

Now read the following sentences, and carefully note that the words printed in italics are Pronouns.

Did *I* not tell *you* to be punctual, Rama ?

Yes, Sir; but *I* missed the train.

Why are *you* crying ? Are *you* afraid of *me* ?

We should always speak the truth.

Let *us* go out for a walk.

EXERCISE 1

Pick out the *Pronouns* in the following sentences and say for what each stands :

1. When the tiger saw the woman, it sprang upon her.

2. The girl lost a bangle, but she found it near her.

3. The child saw a ball and tried to get it.

4. Just listen to him. He must be mad to talk so.

5. Buy them; they are the best mangoes in the shop.

New Simple English Grammar

6. A miser bought a lump of gold. He buried it in a hole.

7. Some boys found a nest in a tree. It was very wonderful. They found five eggs in it.

8. The lark is singing gaily; it loves the bright sun.

9. One day the boy took his breakfast, and ate it by a purling brook.

10. I met a little cottage girl; she was eight years old, she said.

EXERCISE 2

Change some of the *Nouns* into *Pronouns* in the following:

1. The girl sang sweetly. The people listened to the girl. The people liked the girl. The people gave the girl money.

2. These soldiers are wounded. These soldiers must go to hospital. The doctors will heal these soldiers. The doctors will not make the soldiers pay money.

3. A boy saw a mango. The boy wanted the mango. The boy said, "The mango is ripe." The boy took the mango.

4. Rama saw Arjun. Rama called out to Arjun. Arjun answered Rama. Rama and Arjun went along together. I saw Rama and Arjun.

5. I heard a beggar asking for alms. The beggar was very old and weak. I gave the beggar a rupee. The beggar took the rupee and thanked me.

6. I have a little pony. I lent the pony to a lady. The lady rode the pony through the mire.

Kinds of Pronouns

Chapter *12*

Read these sentences :

1. *Did I* not tell *you* to be punctual, Rama ?
2. *We* should always speak the truth.
3. Why are *you* crying ? Are *you* afraid of *me* ?
4. Let *us* go out for a walk.
5. Some men are not honest. *They* steal things.
6. Open this box. It is locked.
7. *I, you, he,* and *she* will do *it* together.

The pronouns in the above sentences stand for the names of persons or things. Such pronouns are called **Personal Pronouns**.

A Pronoun referring to the person *speaking,* is said to be of the **First Person**; as, *I, me, we, us.*

A Pronoun referring to the person *spoken to*, is said to be of the **Second Person**; as; *thou, you.*

A Pronoun referring to the person or thing *spoken of,* is said to be of the **Third Person**; as, *he, him, she, her, it, they, them.*

Read these sentences :

1. I *myself* saw him do it.
2. We will see to it *ourselves*.
3. You *yourself* can best explain.
4. He *himself* said so.
5. She *herself* says so.
6. We saw the President *himself*.
7. The town *itself* is not very large.
8. They *themselves* admitted their guilt.
9. The prisoner hanged *himself*.
10. The horse has hurt *itself*.
11. You express *yourself* very imperfectly.

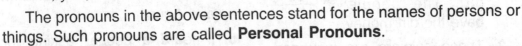

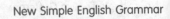

30

New Simple English Grammar

12. I have hurt *myself*.

13. They have got *themselves* into a mess.

14. We often deceive *ourselves*.

It will be seen that the words in italics are used in two ways:

(1) For *emphasis*, with a noun or pronoun, as in sentences, 1, 2, 3, 4, 5, 6, 7, 8. They are then called **Emphasizing Pronouns**.

I myself open the window.

THE OBJECT DENOTES THE SAME
PERSON OR THING AS THE SUBJECT

The fan itself stopped moving.

(2) As *reflexives,* when they are objects of a verb, but refer to the same person as the subject of the verb, as in sentences 9, 10, 11, 12, 13, 14. They are then called **Reflexive Pronouns**.

Whom did the prisoner hang ? .... *himself.*

We see that the prisoner is the doer of the action as well as the receiver of the action.

EXERCISE 1

Pick out the *Pronouns* in the following sentences, and say which are Emphasizing and which Reflexive :

1. I will do it myself.
2. He hurt himself.
3. I posted the letter myself.
4. The Governer himself gave the prize.
5. I blame myself for it.
6. I shut the gate myself.

7. The boys hid themselves.
8. Pray do not inconvenience yourself.
9. You may hurt yourself.
10. She poisoned herself.
11. He set himself a hard task.
12. We seldom see ourselves as others see us.

POINT OUT THE OBJECT OR OBJECTS.

 This is a fan

That is a tree

These are chairs

Those are children

Read these sentences :

1. *This* is a present from my uncle.
2. *These* are merely excuses.
3. *That* is my house.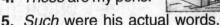
4. *Those* are my pens.
5. *Such* were his actual words.

In the above sentences *this, these, that, those, such* are used to *point out* the object or objects to which they refer, and are therefore called **Demonstrative Pronouns.**

Read these sentences :

1. *Some* say he is mad.
2. *Few* escaped unhurt.
3. *Many* are of that opinion.
4. *All* were drowned.
5. Do good to *others.*
6. *None* but fools have ever believed it.
7. *One* cannot do just as *one* likes.

The Pronouns *some, few, many, all,* etc., refer to people or things in a *vague* and *general* way. They are therefore called **Indefinite Pronouns.**

EXERCISE 2

Pick out the *Demonstrative* and *Indefinite Pronouns* in the following sentences :

1. Can any of you do this sum ?
2. This is my book; that is yours.
3. One hardly knows what to do.
4. None can tell how it happened.
5. Give me one of those.
6. No need to fear that.
7. Some were paid in gold, some in silver.
8. These mangoes are not ripe, send us some ripe ones.
9. One cannot help smiling at what he says.
10. This is certainly a mistake.

New Simple English Grammar

Read these sentences :

1. *Each* of the men received a reward.
2. *Either* of you can go.
3. *Neither* of the accusations is true.

Each, either, neither are used with reference to a number of persons or things *one at a time,* and are called **Distributive Pronouns.**

Read these sentences :

1. *Who* broke this window ?
2. *What* shall we do now ?
3. *Which* would you prefer ?

In the above sentences, the pronouns *who, what* and *which,* not only stand instead of nouns, but also *ask questions.* Pronouns used for asking questions are called **Interrogative Pronouns.**

EXERCISE 3

Pick out the *Interrogative Pronouns* in the following sentences:

1. Which is your uncle's house ?
2. Who is there ?
3. What is the matter ?
4. Who made the top score ?
5. Which will you take ?
6. What is the news ?
7. What are those marks on your shirt ?
8. Whom do you want ?
9. To whom were you speaking?
10. Whose is this ?

EXERCISE 4

Write down three sentences, using the pronouns *who, which* and *what* as *Interrogative Pronouns.*

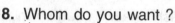

....

....

....

Examine the work done by each word in *italics* in the following pairs of sentences:

1. *This* boy is lazy. (Dem. Adj.)

   This is a present from my uncle. (Dem. Pron.)

2. What is *that* noise ? (Dem. Adj.)

   Who was *that* ? (Dem. Pron.)

3. *What* books have you read ? (Interrog. Adj.)

   What does he want ? (Interrog. Pron.)

4. *Which* way shall we go ? (Interrog. Adj.)

   Which is your book? (Interrog. Pron.)

It will be seen that many of the words used as Pronouns in this chapter do the work of Adjectives when they are placed before nouns.

EXERCISE 5

Pick out the *Pronouns* in the following sentences, and tell the kind of each pronoun :

1. The female lion is called a lioness. She has no mane.

2. The camel is a beast of burden. It is used to carry goods across the desert.

3. He has lost his dog and cannot find it.

4. Somebody has stolen my watch.

5. I wish I hadn't cried so much.

6. Both cars are good : but this is better than that.

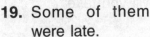

7. There were doors all round the hall, but they were all locked.

8. May I take this ?

9. I want that ball; it is mine.

10. All answered their names.

11. Some believed the story, others did not.

12. The old man often talks to himself.

13. Hallo, Rama, is this ball yours ?

14. None of the boys seemed to like him.

15. Put them down.

16. Most people like her.

17. Has anybody seen my ball ?

18. Each of us has two mangoes.

19. Some of them were late.

20. What did they say ?

21. Few have such a chance.

22. Neither of them knows the story.

23. Either of you can go.

Read these sentences :

1. I know that boy *who* is coming.
2. Bring me the letters *which* the postman left.
3. This is the house *that* Jack built.

In the above sentences, the Pronouns *who, which* and *that,* not only stand instead of nouns, but also join the parts of the sentences together. Instead of saying "I know that boy. That boy is coming," we say "I know that boy *who* is coming," and so make only one sentence.

These pronouns, *who, which* and *that,* used as shown above, are called **Relative Pronouns**, because they *relate* or refer to a noun which has gone before.

The noun to which a relative pronoun refers or relates is called its **Antecedent** (which means *going before*).

It will be noticed that in sentence 1 the antecedent of *who* is *boy.* In sentence 2 the antecedent of *which* is *letters.* In sentence 3 the antecedent of *that* is *house.*

Note: In the sentence "I don't know *what* you mean," the word *what* is a relative pronoun. It will be seen that the antecedent of the relative pronoun *what* is not expressed.

EXERCISE 1

Pick out the *Relative Pronouns* in the following sentences:

1. The cat killed the rat that ate the corn.
2. I know what you mean.
3. Where is the book which I gave you?
4. God helps those who help themselves.
5. Listen to what I say.
6. I have seen the bird which you describe.
7. I know the man who lives here.
8. Here is the book that you lent me.
9. He remembers what he reads.

10. I have found the pen which I lost.
11. Take anything that you like.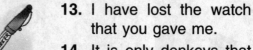
12. Give me what you can.

13. I have lost the watch that you gave me.
14. It is only donkeys that bray.

EXERCISE 2

Write down four sentences, each containing a *Relative Pronoun*.

EXERCISE 3

Pick out the *Interrogative* and the *Relative Pronouns* in the following sentences:

1. The dog which I recently bought is an Alsatian.
2. Which is your book ?
3. What shall we do today ?
4. He found what he was looking for.
5. What was in the desk?

6. Halt ! Who goes there ?
7. The answer which you gave is not right.
8. This is the juggler whom we saw yesterday.
9. Who is knocking at the door ?
10. Whom did you see there ?
11. The man who is honest is trusted.

EXERCISE 4

Pick out the *Pronouns* in the following sentences, and tell the class to which each belongs :

1. That is the boy about whom I spoke.
2. Whose pen is this ? Which of you has lost it ?
3. I do not think he understands what you mean.
4. Who is the man to whom you were talking, and what does he want ?
5. We all want what we have not got.

6. I warned them that they would bring trouble on themselves.
7. To whom are you writing ?
8. What do you suppose will happen to the person who did this?
9. One should try to see oneself as others do.
10. He that hath not served knoweth not how to command.

Chapter 14

The Preposition

Read these sentences :

1. The book is *on* the desk.
2. The book is *under* the desk.
3. The book is *near* the desk.
4. The book is *in* the desk.
5. The book is *beside* the desk.
6. The book is *above* the desk.
7. The book is *below* the desk.

Each of the above sentences contains a word that shows the *relation between* the book and the desk. Such words are called **Prepositions**.

Now examine the following sentences :

1. He lives *near* us.
2. He came *with* me.
3. The letter is *from* him.
4. I do not believe *in* them.
5. There is a wall *round* it.

In these sentences you see the Prepositions used with pronouns.

> A **Preposition** is a word placed before a noun (or a pronoun) to show in what relation the person or thing denoted by the noun stands to something else.

EXERCISE 1

Pick out the *Prepositions* in the following sentences :

1. Father is not at home.
2. Let us go for a walk.
3. He has eaten nothing since yesterday.
4. The boy fell off his bike.
5. What is that in your hand ?
6. He was among the crowd.

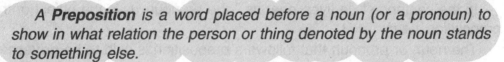

7. I gave fifty rupees for it.
8. Let us´ walk along the shore.
9. I don't know anything about it.
10. The policeman is on duty.

EXERCISE 2

Pick out the *Prepositions* in the following sentences :

1. Little Jack Horner sat in a corner.
2. Old Mother Hubbard, she went to the cupboard.
3. The lion and the unicorn fought for the crown.
4. Humpty Dumpty sat on a wall.
5. Wee Willie Winkie runs through the town.

6. She sat by the fire, and told me a tale.
7. Rain, rain, go to Spain, and never come back again !
8. A fair little girl sat under a tree.
9. "Will you walk into my parlour?" said the spider to the fly.
10. Into the street the Piper stepped.

You will remember that a transitive verb must have an object. If we say "The winner will receive", it is clear that the sentence is not complete. The winner must receive *something*, or he does not receive. The verb must have an object, or the sentence is not complete.

In the same way, *a preposition must have an object*. If we say "The letter is from," it is clear that the sentence is not complete. The letter must be from somebody (or some place). The preposition must have an object or the sentence is not complete. We must say "The letter is from Rama" or "The letter is from Mumbai," or something similar.

If you look at the first seven sentences in this chapter, you will see that the noun *desk* is, in each case, the object of the preposition.

In the sentence "He lives *near* us," the pronoun *us* is the object of the preposition *near*.

The noun or pronoun that follows a preposition is said to be **governed by the preposition**, and is called its **Object**.

EXERCISE 3

Pick out each *Preposition* and its *Object* in the following sentences:

1. He is blind in one eye.
2. His house is near mine.
3. He returned after a year.
4. Have you seen a rose without a thorn ?
5. What are you looking at ?
6. What is he talking about ?

7. She is weak in arithmetic.
8. The horse jumped over the hedge.
9. She spoke in a whisper.
10. The boy climbed up the ladder.

EXERCISE 4

Fill up the blanks with suitable _Prepositions_ :

1. The horse is .... the stable.

2. He got angry .... me.

3. Do not go .... the river.

4. He jumped ....the gate.

5. He sat ....a chair.

6. The coolie saw a snake .... his foot.

7. The sky is .... our heads.

8. We took shelter .... a tree.

9. You will be punished .... your fault.

10. It is raining; do not go .... your umbrella.

EXERCISE 5

Fill up the blanks with suitable _Prepositions_ :

1. How far is your school .... here ?

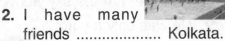

2. I have many friends .... Kolkata.

3. We do not work .... holidays.

4. I wash my hands .... soap and water.

5. Many thanks .... your invitation.

6. Have you been waiting long .... me ?

7. That man walks .... a stick.

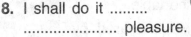

8. I shall do it .... pleasure.

9. Which is the nearest way .... the Town Hall ?

10. My mother is suffering .... fever.

Examine these sentences :

1. The rocket went _up_.

2. The little boy climbed _up_ the ladder.

In the first sentence the word _up_ adds something to the meaning of the verb _go_. It is therefore an adverb modifying the verb _go_.

In the second sentence the word _up_ shows the relation between the "climbing of the little boy" and "the ladder". It is therefore a preposition governing the noun _ladder_.

Now examine the following pairs of sentences. You will see that many words which are Prepositions when they are used *with a noun or pronoun*, are Adverbs when they modify a word in the sentence.

1. There are thieves *about*. (Adv.)
   We often talk *about* you. (Prep.)
2. I have heard that *before*. (Adv.)
   He arrived there a few minutes *before* me. (Prep.)
3. He lives close *by*. (Adv.)
   I require my new coat *by* Monday. (Prep.)
4. The train is *in*. (Adv.)
   He is *in* bad health. (Prep.)
5. The flowers are coming *on*. (Adv.)
   I hope to see you *on* Tuesday. (Prep.)

EXERCISE 6

Work in pairs and decide which of the words in italics are *Adverbs* and which *Prepositions*.

1. *After* a month he returned.
2. She arrived soon *after*.
3. Let us move *on*.
4. The book lies *on* the table.
5. He is feared by all *below* him.
6. Come down *below*.
7. The roof is *above* us.
8. He looked at the sky *above*.
9. He was only a yard *off* me.
10. Suddenly one of the wheels came off.

Chapter 15

The Conjunction

Read these sentences :

1. Rama has gone **and** Arjun has come.
2. Do your work **or** I shall punish you.
3. I called him **but** he did not hear me.

The word **and** joins the two groups of words *Rama has gone* and *Arjun has come.*

The word **or** joins the word group *Do your work* to the word group *I shall punish you.*

The word **but** joins the word group *I called him* to the word group *He did not hear me.*

These words **and, or, but,** which are used *to join* one group of words to another, are called **Conjunctions**. (Latin *con,* together, and *junctus,* joined.)

Sometimes a Conjunction merely joins *words;* as,

Two *and* two make four.

Here the Conjunction *and* joins the words *Two* and *two.*

A **Conjunction** *is a word that joins words* or *groups of words* togehter.

The following sentences contain additional examples of Conjunctions:

I did not come **because** you did not call me.
Give me to drink, **else** I shall die of thirst.
You will get the prize **if** you deserve it.
Do not go **before** I come.
I hear **that** your brother is in London.

Will you wait **till** I return ?
He deserved to succeed **for** he worked hard.
He asked **whether** he might have a holiday.
I will stay **until** you return.

He was sorry **after** he had done it.
Unless you tell me the truth, I shall punish you.
He finished first **though** he began late.

Since you say so, I must believe it.

As he was not there, I spoke to his brother.

When I was younger I thought so.

They are poor *yet* cheerful.

The bag was heavy *therefore* I could not carry it.

I missed the train *although* I walked fast.

The earth is larger *than* the moon [is large].

Some Conjunctions are used in pairs; as,

Both — and. We *both* love *and* honour him.

Either — or. Either take it *or* leave it.

Neither — nor. It is *neither* useful *nor* ornamental.

Whether — or. I do not care *whether* you go *or* stay.

Not only — but also. Not only is he foolish, *but also* obstinate.

Conjunctions which are thus used in pairs are called **Correlative Conjunctions** or merely **Correlatives**.

EXERCISE 1

Pick out the *Conjunctions* in the following sentences:

1. The bag was heavy therefore I could not carry it.
2. He will help you if you ask him.
3. He will never succeed although he works hard.
4. Ask him whether he wishes to go or not.
5. You can come if you like.
6. Either you or I must go.
7. Don't answer unless you know.
8. There dwelt a miller hale and bold.
9. His petticoats now George cast off, for he was four years old.
10. I don't know whether he is here or not.

EXERCISE 2

Fill each blank in the following sentences with an appropriate *Conjunction*:

1. Will you kindly wait .... I return ?
2. Catch me .... you can.
3. The grasshopper would not have starved in winter .... she had not been lazy all the summer.
4. We saw the lightning .... we heard the thunder.

5. I will go away .... you fail.

6. The tortoise beat the hare .... the hare was the swifter of the two.

7. I shall be surprised ....

8. Cats can climb trees, ... dogs cannot.

9. He has succeeded better .... he hoped.

10. We can travel by land .... by water.

EXERCISE 3

Work with another student and join the following pairs of sentences together by means of a suitable *Conjunction*:

1. He is rich. He is not happy.

2. You must be quiet. You must leave the room.

3. He forgave him. He was penitent.

4. He put in his thumb. He pulled out a plum.

5. Rama works hard. Hari is idle.

6. He was afraid of being late. He ran.

7. I stumbled. I was going downstairs.

8. Balu made twelve runs. He was caught at the wicket.

9. He did not succeed. He worked hard.

10. I lost the prize. I tried my best.

11. This mango is large. This mango is sweet.

12. Mother is at home. Father is at home.

13. Rama may be in the house. Rama may be in the garden.

14. Hari did not come. He did not send a letter.

15. You are tall. My brother is taller.

EXERCISE 4

Frame sentences containing the following *Conjunctions*:

but, or, and, therefore, because, till, after.

....

....

....

....

....

Chapter 16

The Interjection

Read these sentences :

1. *Hurrah !* Our side has won.
2. *Alas !* Our side has lost.
3. *Hush !* I hear someone coming.
4. *Bravo,* Rama ! Well hit.
5. *Hallo,* Govind ! How are you ?

6. *Ouch !* You are hurting me.
7. *Wow !* What a wonderful painting !
8. *Hey !* Where are you going ?
9. *Ah !* that's the excuse every lazy boy makes.
10. *Oh !* What a beautiful rose !

Each of the above sentences begins with a word which is used *to show some feeling* of the mind.

The word *Hurrah* is really a noise made to express pleasure.

The word *alas* is used to express sadness. (Today this word is rarely used in spoken English.)

Sh (or *shh/ Ssh*) is used to tell somebody to be quiet.

Bravo is used to show approval of something.

Hallo (or Hello/ Hullo) is used when meeting or greeting someone or when starting a conversation on the phone. We also use this word to attract someone's attention.

Ouch is a cry expressing sudden pain.

Wow is used to express great surprise or admiration.

Hey is used to attract someone's attention or to express interest, surprise or anger.

Ah expresses surprise, pleasure, admiration, etc.

Oh expresses surprise, fear, pleasure, etc.

Words such as these are called **Interjections**.

An **Interjection** is a word used to expess some strong feeling of the mind.

Such words are called **Interjections.**

An **Interjection** is a word used merely to express some sudden feeling of the mind.

The word *Interjection* comes from the Latin *inter*, between, and *jactus*, thrown. It is a word thrown into the sentence and does not really form a part of it.

EXERCISE

A. Fill in the blanks with suitable *Interjections* :

1. .... ! You have done well.
2. .... ! You will wake the baby.
3. .... ! India has won !
4. .... ! What are you doing there ?
5. .... ! You have stepped on my foot !
6. .... ! What a strong man !

B. Imagine you are watching a cricket match or some other interesting or exciting programme on TV. What interjections would you use to express your feelings ? Write five sentences, using an *Interjection* in each.

....

....

....

....

....

....

We have now dealt with the eight different classes of words, or, as they are called, the eight **Parts of Speech**. *All* words must belong to one of these eight classes.

But do not think that a word must always belong to the same class.

A word is not *born,* so to speak, a certain part of speech. It *becomes a* part of speech, according to how it is *used* in a sentence; or, in other words, according to the *work it does.*

Hence if I asked you what part of speech the word *that* is, your reply should be, "That depends on how it is *used* in a sentence."

In the sentence "I know that boy", *that* is an adjective.

In the sentence "Don't do that," *that* is a pronoun.

In the sentence "I was told that he was dead," *that* is a conjunction.

In the following exercises, therefore, say to what part of speech a word belongs after carefully noticing *how it is used.*

EXERCISE 1

Which of the italicised words are *Nouns* and which *Verbs* ? Give reasons for your answer.

1. I knew him by his *walk.*
2. I would rather *walk* than run.
3. It was a good *catch.*
4. Cats *catch* mice.
5. We generally *breakfast* on bread and butter.

6. He ate a good *breakfast.*
7. Our old *cook* died yesterday.
8. I sometimes *cook* my dinner.
9. Some bad boys *smoke* cigarettes.
10. There is no *smoke* without fire.

EXERCISE 2

Which of the italicised words are *Nouns* and which *Adjectives* ? Give reasons for your answer.

1. *Gold* is a precious metal.
2. My friend has a *gold* watch.
3. The child has caught *cold*.

4. It is a *cold* evening.
5. Few people can keep a *secret*.
6. The room has a *secret* door.

EXERCISE 3

Which of the italicised words are *Adjectives* and which *Adverbs*? Give reasons for your answer.

1. Men who work *hard* enjoy life fully.
2. I know *better*.
3. I think yours is a *better* plan.
4. Where shall we go *next* ?
5. I will see you *next* Monday.
6. *Most* people think so.

7. What *most* annoys me is his obstinacy.
8. I assure you, you will have *little* trouble.
9. It matters *little* what he says.
10. Do not speak so *loud*.

EXERCISE 4

Which of the italicised words are *Adverbs* and which *Prepositions*? Give reasons for your answer.

1. He arrived *before* me.
2. I could not come *before*.
3. The book lies *on* the table.

4. Let us move *on*.
5. The path leads *through* the woods.

6. I have read the book *through*.
7. Sit *by* me.
8. Stand *by*.
9. Let us stand *behind*.
10. There is someone *behind* the door.

EXERCISE 5

Which of the italicised words are *Prepositions* and which *Conjunctions*? Give reasons for your answer.

1. He went *after* I came.
2. The dog ran *after* the cat.
3. We shall stay here *till* you return.

4. Stay *till* Monday.
5. He died *for* his country.
6. I cannot give you anything, *for* I have nothing.

7. Look *before* you leap.

8. He stood *before* the door.

9. We have not seen him *since* yesterday.

10. He has been here *since* you left.

Say what *Part of Speech* is each of the italicised words :

1. He went away *before* I came.
2. I have seen you *before*.
3. He came *before* the appointed time.
4. He boasts too *much*.
5. There is *much* sense in what she says.
6. *Much* of it is true.
7. His house is *near* the temple.
8. Draw *near* and listen.
9. He is a *near* relation.
10. You know well *enough* what I mean.

To *Parse* a word is to tell what part of speech it is.

Let us *parse* the words in italics in the following sentences :

A *crow once stole* a *big piece of* cheese.

He came *after* we left.

crow :   a Noun, because it is a name.

once :   an Adverb modifying the verb *stole*, because it tells us *when* a crow *stole*.

stole :   a Verb, because it *says* what a crow *did*.

big :   an Adjective qualifying the noun *piece*, because it goes with the noun *piece* to *describe it*.

of :   a Preposition governing the noun *cheese*, because it shows the relation between two things, *piece* and *cheese*.

he :   a Pronoun, because it is used instead of a noun.

after :   a Conjunction, because it joins the sentence "He came" to the sentence "We left."

***Parse* the words in italics in the following sentences :**

1. We will go *along this* road.
2. The boys came *along* and their master came *after*.
3. *Round* went the wheels.
4. There was a *round* table *in* the room.
5. They *call* him Bapu.

Chapter 18

Number

Examine the following sentences :

1. Please give me your *book*.
2. Please give me your *books*.

The Noun *book* stands for only *one* thing. It is, therefore, said to be in the **Singular Number**.

> Any Noun standing for *one* person or thing is said to be in the **Singular Number; as,**
> boy, man, donkey, chair, desk.

The Noun *books* stands for *more than one* thing. It is, therefore, said to be in the **Plural Number**.

> Any Noun standing for *more than one* person or thing is said to be in the **Plural Number; as,**
> boys, men, donkeys, chairs, desks.

EXERCISE 1

Point out the Nouns in these sentences. State about each Noun whether it stands for one thing (or person), or more than one thing (or person).

1. The boys are writing in copybooks.
2. A little girl is playing with her friends.
3. Cows give milk.
4. There are many houses in this street.
5. There are five cups on the table.
6. The room has four walls and two doors.
7. All the inkpots are new.
8. I have three balls, but only two bats.
9. There are seven days in a week.
10. This book has sixty-four pages.

Sunday, Monday, Tuesday, Wednesday, Thursday, Friday, Saturday

Most Nouns form their plurals by adding –s to the singular; as,

boy, boys; girl, girls; dog, dogs; horse, horses; chair, chairs.

Some Nouns, however, form their plurals differently;

(1) By adding **–es**, if the noun ends in **–s, –sh, –ch** (soft) or **–x** ; as,

bus, buses; glass, glasses; brush, brushes; bench, benches; box, boxes

(2) By changing **y** into **i** and adding **–es**, if the i comes after a consonant ; as,

pony → ponies; lady → ladies; fly → flies; city → cities.

(3) *By changing* **–f** *into* **–v** *and adding* **–es**; as,

thief → thieves; knife → knives; calf → calves; leaf → leaves.

(4) *By a change of vowel;* as,

man → men; woman → women; foot → feet; tooth → teeth;
mouse → mice.

(5) *By adding* **en**; as,

ox → oxen; child → children.

The nouns **sheep, dear** and **fish** do not change in the plural. The form **fishes** can be used to refer to different kinds of fish.

The usual plural of **person** is **people**. The form **persons** is sometimes used in official language.

EXERCISE 2

Write the *Singular* of each of the following :

mice, flies, watches, children, houses, cities, matches, branches.

EXERCISE 3

Write the *Plural* of each of the following :

baby, branch, bush, wolf, army, loaf, goose, face, wife, child, fox, buffalo, potato.

Examine the following pairs of sentences. What do you notice ?

{ This mango *is* ripe.
{ These mangoes *are* ripe.

These
mangoes
are ripe.

{ The child *has* toys.
{ The children *have* toys.

{ The cock *is* crowing
{ The cocks *are* crowing.

{ The boy sentences *plays* every
evening.

{ The boy *was* there.
{ The boys *were* there.

{ The boys *play* every
evening.

{ The boy *was* playing.
{ The boys *were* playing.

{ The man *does* his work well.
{ The men *do* their work well.

When we change a singular subject into the plural, the verb also changes.

EXERCISE 4

Fill in the blank spaces with "is" or "are" :

1. The child .... happy.   2. The children ....
happy.

3. My books...................... stolen.
4. The child...................... there.

5. All boys .... fond of play.

Fill in the blank spaces with "was" or "were" :

1. All the schools .... open yesterday.
2. The books .... in the desk.
3. Only one boy .... absent.

4. Some boys .... inattentive.
5. My sister .... watching a video.

Fill in the blank spaces with "has" or "have" :

1. My uncle .... a computer.
2. My boots .... thick soles.

3. Cats .... sharp claws.
4. The horse .... a tail.
5. Cows .... horns.

Fill in the blanks with "is" or "are", "has" or "have" :

1. Jane .... a little girl.
2. These children .... no toys to play with.
3. The cow .... two horns.

4. This cassette .... new.
5. Coconut trees .... very useful.

Fill in the blanks :

1. The lion .... (Roar or roars ?)
2. The birds .... (Sing or sings ?)

3. This boot .... me. (Hurt or hurts ?)
4. The cow .... grass. (Eat or eats ?)
5. Ducks .... to swim in a pond. (Like or likes ?)

EXERCISE 9

Change the *Subject* into *Plural*, making at the same time other necessary changes :

1. The boy is playing.
2. The book was in the desk.
3. The cat has sharp claws.
4. A bird is singing on that tree.
5. The boy speaks English.
6. The girl sings sweetly.
7. This mango is ripe.
8. A bad boy tells lies.
9. The owl sleeps in the day-time.
10. The rabbit has a short tail.

EXERCISE 10

Change the *Subject* into *Singular*, making at the same time other necessary changes :

1. These oranges are very sweet.
2. Two boys were absent yesterday.
3. Those mangoes are not ripe.
4. My sisters speak English.
5. Good children are liked by all.
6. The windows facing the street are broken.
7. The thieves were arrested last night.
8. There are five benches in this room.
9. The boys are writing in their copybooks.
10. Some boys were in the playground.

Like a Noun, a Pronoun is said to be in the Singular Number when it stands for *one* person or thing, and in the Plural Number when it stands for *more than one* person or thing.

Read the following sentences :
1. The *boy* plays well.
2. *Mary* has a little lamb.
3. The *box* is made of wood.
4. The *child* is ill.

The Noun *boy* is the name of a *male*. It is therefore said to be of the **Masculine Gender**.

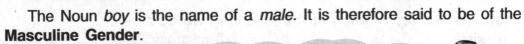

> A Noun that is the name of any male person or animal is said to be of the **Masculine Gender;** as,
> man, uncle, lion, bull.

The Noun *Mary* is the name of a *female*. It is therefore said to be of the **Feminine Gender**.

> A Noun that is the name of any female person or animal is said to be of the **Feminine Gender;** as,
> woman, aunt, lioness, cow.

The Noun *box* is the name of a thing *without life.* It is therefore said to be of the **Neuter Gender**, that is, of *neither* gender.

> A Noun which stands for the name of a thing without life is said to be of the **Neuter Gender;** as,
> desk, chair, ball, knife.

The Noun *child* may be used both for a male child and a female child. It is therefore said to be of the **Common Gender**.

> Nouns which may be used both for males and females are said to be of the **Common Gender;** as,
> friend, cousin, pupil, person, parent.

(i) Some Feminine Nouns are formed from the Masculine *by adding the suffix* **-ess** (sometimes with a slight change) or **-ine**; as,

lion → lioness; shepherd → shepherdess; actor → actress;
hero → heroine.

(ii) Some Feminine Nouns are formed from the Masculine *by changing the prefix;* as,

cock-sparrow → hen-sparrow; he-goat → she-goat;
manservant → maidservant.

(iii) Many Nouns have *different words* for the Masculine and the Feminine; as,

boy → girl; uncle → aunt; king → queen; bull → cow; cock → hen.

EXERCISE

State the *Gender* of each of the following words :

(i) sister	(xi) mistress ....
(ii) dog	(xii) servant ....
(iii) mother	(xiii) nephew ....
(iv) actor	(xiv) slave ....
(v) tigress	(xv) flower ....
(vi) master	(xvi) baby ....
(vii) actress	(xvii) ox ....
(viii) tree	(xviii) prince ....
(ix) emperor...................................	(xix) pupil ....
(x) cook	(xx) chair ....

Examine the sentence :

John hit Tom.

What is the relation of the noun *John* to the verb *hit* ? The noun *John* stands as the Subject of the verb *hit.*

When the noun *John* stands as the Subject of a verb, it is said to be in the *naming relation* or **Nominative Case**.

> Any noun (or pronoun) that is the Subject of a verb is said to be in the **Nominative Case; as,**
>
> The *police* arrested the thief.
> (*Who* arrested ? — The *police*.)
> The *pot* was broken by Hari.
> (*What* was broken ? — The *pot*.)
> *He* bought a digital watch.
> (*Who* bought ? — *He*.)

Examine the sentence :

Tom hit John.

What is the relation of the noun *John* to the verb *hit* ? The noun *John* stands as the Object of the verb *hit.*

When the noun *John* stands as the Object of a verb, it is said to be in the **Objective Case.**

> Any noun (or pronoun) that is the Object of a verb is said to be in the **Objective Case; as,**
>
> The police arrested the *thief.*
> (*Whom* did the police arrest ? — The *thief*.)
> *He* bought a silver watch.
> (*What* did he buy ? — A silver *watch*.)
> The Objective Case is sometimes called the **Accusative Case.**

EXERCISE 1

In each of the following sentences, pick out the nouns in the *Nominative Case*:

1. The foolish old crow tried to sing.

2. Few cats like cold water.

3. Rama married Sita.

4. Sita married Rama.
5. My uncle lives in the next house.
6. Humpty Dumpty sat on a wall.
7. Lakshmi lost her ring.

8. Kolkata stands on the banks of the Hooghli.
9. The lazy boy was punished.
10. Gopal wants to go home.

EXERCISE 2

Pick out the nouns in the *Objective Case* in the following sentences:

1. Putli found a ring.
2. The mongoose eats snakes.
3. Snakes fear the mongoose.
4. The village master taught his little school.
5. Sir Ralph the Rover tore his hair.
6. Little Bo-Peep has lost her sheep.
7. Aladdin had a wonderful lamp.
8. I met a little cottage girl.
9. Simple Simon met a pieman.
10. I saw him.
11. He saw me.
12. Do you know the way ?

Nouns and pronouns following Prepositions are also in the Objective Case; as,

The dog ran across the *road.*

He arrived before *me.*

Examine the sentences :

1. The dog bit the monkey.　　2. The monkey bit the dog.

In sentence 1 the noun **dog** is the Subject of the verb **bit,** and is in the Nominative case.

In sentence 2 the noun **dog** is the Object of the verb **bit,** and is in the Objective case.

Again in sentence 2 the noun **monkey** is the Subject of the verb **bit,** and is in the Nominative case.

In sentence 1 the noun **monkey** is the Object of the verb **bit,** and is in the Objective case.

We thus see that the Nominative and Objective cases of Nouns are alike in form, but are known by their position in the sentence and the sense.

The Nominative generally comes *before* the verb, and the Objective *after* it.

Now examine the following sentences :

1. He struck me.　　2. I struck him.

It will be noticed that the Nominative and Objective cases of Pronouns are indicated *by a change of form.* Thus *he,* Nominative, changes in form and becomes *him* in the Objective; similarly *I,* Nominative, changes in form and becomes *me* in the Objective.

Chapter 21

Case (Contd.)

Look at the following sentences :

1. This is *Rama's* book.
2. Is that your *brother's* bat ?
3. My *uncle's* house is a long way from here.

In each of these sentences we see a pair of nouns, one of which is the name of the possessor and the other the name of the thing possessed.

A noun (or pronoun) used *to show possession* is said to be in the **Possessive Case**.

In the above sentences each of the nouns, *Rama's, brother's, uncle's*, is in the Possessive Case.

The Possessive Case is sometimes called the **Genetive Case**.

The Possessive answers the question, *Whose* ?

Whose book is this ? — *Rama's.*

The meaning of the Possessive Case may be expressed by means of the preposition *of* with the objective case after it. Thus, for "My uncle's house" we may say, "The house of my uncle."

Now read the following sentences :

1. *Shirin's* mother is ill.
2. The *horse's* mane is long.
3. The *bee's* sting is painful.

In these sentences the nouns in the Possessive Case are in the singular number, and the Possessive Case is formed *by adding an apostrophe* (') *and a s.*

Now examine the nouns in the Possessive Case in the following sentences :

1. Many *boys'* books are lost.
2. All these *horses'* feet are shod.
3. We saw rows of *soldiers'* tents.

As you see, the nouns in the Possessive Case are here in the plural number. *As the plural nouns themselves end in s*, only the apostrophe (') is used, and not another *s*.

Examine these sentences :

1. *Men's* lives are short.
2. The *children's* toys are broken.
3. These *oxen's* humps are large.

In these sentences the nouns in the possessive case are in the plural number *but do not end in s.* Therefore the apostrophe (') and s are used (as in the singular).

The Possessive Case is chiefly used when the noun denotes some *living* thing. Thus we say :

Children's toys; horses' feet; Mary's book.

When the noun denotes anything *without life*, possession is generally expressed by the preposition *of*, followed by the noun in the objective case as,

The leg of the table [*not,* the table's leg.]

The cover of the book [*not,* the book's cover.]

But the Possessive Case is used with nouns denoting *time, space,* or *weight;* as.

A *day's* march; a *week's* holiday; a *metre's* length; a *kilo's* weight.

EXERCISE 1

Pick out the nouns in the *Possessive Case* in the following sentences:

1. The children found a bird's nest.
2. Tom attends a boys' school.
3. The children's clothes are new.
4. The ladies' sarees were beautiful.
5. The girl's voice is sweet.
6. The farmer's work is done.
7. The baby's doll is lost.
8. The boy's uncle is here.
9. This is Kishore's umbrella.

EXERCISE 2

Write the *Possessive case, singular* and *Plural*, of the following nouns:

baby, child, boy, lady, man, sheep, monkey, ox.

PERSON SPOKEN TO OR ADDRESSED.

Look at the sentence :

Stand there, *Rama.*

Here *Rama* is the name of the person *spoken to* or *addressed*. It is, therefore, said to be in the **Vocative Case**. The Vocative Case is also called the **Nominative of Address.**

Further examples of the Nominative of Address :

1. Come on, *boys.*
2. Come into the garden, *Maud.*
3. Drink, pretty *creature*, drink.
4. O *Mary,* go and call the cattle home.

EXERCISE 3

In the following sentences pick out the nouns and tell the *Number, Gender* and *Case* of each :

1. Hari's books are in the desk.
2. Come away, children.
3. The fox came to the farmer's gate.
4. A mad dog bit my pony.
5. The woman shook her head.
6. The boy's coat is torn.
7. The cow loves her calf.
8. The boys made great noise.
9. The farmer's wife jumped out of bed.
10. He wrote a letter to his uncle.
11. My boy, you are mistaken.
12. Hari's knife is blunt.
13. Radha is milking the cow.
14. The children have read the story of Ali Baba.
15. Cinderella's slippers were made of glass.
16. Camels carry heavy burdens.
17. The little girl has a sweet voice.
18. We boil water in a kettle.
19. The noise frightened the child.
20. A mouse awakened a lion from sleep.

Chapter 22

Comparison of Adjectives

Examine the following sentences :
1. That man is *rich*.
2. My uncle is *richer* than him.
3. My father is the *richest* man in the town.

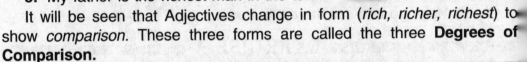

It will be seen that Adjectives change in form (*rich, richer, richest*) to show *comparison*. These three forms are called the three **Degrees of Comparison.**

> The Simple form of the adjective is called the **Positive Degree**; as, *rich*.
> When comparing *two* objects and saying that one possesses a certain quality in a greater degree than the other, we use the *comparative* form of the adjective. We call *richer* the **Comparative Degree** of *rich*.
> When we say that a certain object possesses a quality in the greater degree of all that are being compared, we use the *superlative* form of the adjective; hence the superlative form of the adjective is used when comparing *more than two* objects. We call *richest* the **Superlative Degree** of *rich*.

Examine how the Degrees of Comparison of the following adjectives are formed :

	Positive	*Comparative*	*Superlative*
(1)	Tall	taller	tallest
	Short	shorter	shortest
	Bold	bolder	boldest
	Young	younger	youngest
(2)	Noble	nobler	noblest
	Fine	finer	finest
	Brave	braver	bravest
	Large	larger	largest
(3)	Heavy	heavier	heaviest
	Pretty	prettier	prettiest
	Happy	happier	happiest
	Merry	marrier	merriest
(4)	Fat	fatter	fattest
	Big	bigger	biggest
	Sad	sadder	saddest
	Red	redder	reddest

New Simple English Grammar

(1) The Comparative is usually formed by adding –er to the Positive, and the Superlative is usually formed by adding –est to the Positive.

(2) When the Positive ends in –e, only –r and –st are added.

(3) When the Positive ends in –y with a consonant before it, –y is changed into –i before –er and –est.

(4) When the Positive is a word of one syllable and ends in a single consonant with a short vowel before it, the consonant is doubled before –er and –est.

Most two-syllable adjectives and longer adjectives are compared by prefixing **more** and **most**; as,

Positive	Comparative	Superlative
Tired	more tired	most tired
Active	more active	most active
Beautiful	more beautiful	most beautiful
Interesting	more interesting	most interesting

Do not combine both modes of comparison, and say *more shorter, most shortest.*

There are a few adjectives which are compared *irregularly:*

Positive	Comparative	Superlative
Good	better	best
Bad	worse	worst
Little	less	least
Many	more	most
Much	more	most
Late	{ latter later	{ last latest
Old	{ older elder	{ oldest eldest
Far	farther	farthest

Notice the distinction in the use of *older* and *elder, oldest* and *eldest.*

He is *older* than I am.

He is my *elder* brother.

He is the *oldest* man in the village.

His *eldest* son is sixty years old.

Elder and *oldest* are normally used when comparing members of a family. They go only before nouns.

EXERCISE 1

Give the *Comparative* and *Superlative degrees* of the following Adjectives

Friendly	gay	small
cold	able	pleasant
dull	hot	dry
evil	weak	bright
lazy	idle	handsome
lovely	wonderful	useful
holy	severe	narrow
wise	high	thick
thin	deep	proud
clean	lucky	dangerous

EXERCISE 2

Supply the proper form (*Comparative* or *Superlative*) of the Adjective

1. *Idle.* — Hari is the .... boy in the class.
2. *Pretty.* — Her doll is .... than yours.
3. *Rich.* — He is the .... man in our town.
4. *Bad.* — He is the .... boy of the two.
5. *Light.* — Silver is .... than gold.
6. *Useful.* — Iron is .... than any other metal.
7. *Little.* — That is the .... price I can take.
8. *Tall.* — He is the .... of the two.
9. *Tall.* — Abdul is the .... boy in the school.
10. *Large.* — Of the two mangoes this is the ....

Adjectives in the Comparative Degree are followed by *than;* as,
Sri Lanka is smaller *than* India.

But a few comparatives are followed by *to* instead of *than;* as,
Hari is *inferior to* Rama in intelligence.

This pearl is *superior to* that.

He is *junior to* Hari.

All his classmates are *senior to* him.

The demonstrative adjectives, *this* and *that*, have plural forms, *these* and *those*. Thus we say : *this* book, but *these* boys; *that* man, but *those* men.

Each, every, either, neither, when used as adjectives, go with singular nouns; as,

Each boy must take his turn.

Every boy was punished.

Either pen will do.

Neither knife is of any use.

Chapter 23

The Articles

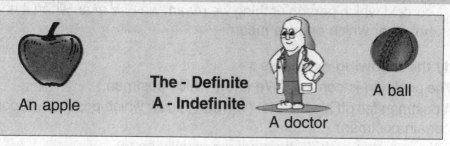

An apple

The - Definite
A - Indefinite

A doctor

A ball

Examine the use of *a* (or *an*) and *the* in the following :

The words *the* and *a* (or *an*) are called ***Articles.***

The word *the* is called the ***Definite Article,*** because it points out some particular person or thing.

I returned ***the*** pen. (*i.e.* some particular pen)

The word a (or *an*) is called the Indefinite Article, because it leaves *indefinite* the person or thing talked about.

I want ***a*** pen (*i.e.* any pen)

The form ***an*** is used, instead of a, before a word beginning with a vowel sound or a silent ***h.***

an axe, *an* enemy, *an* inkpad, *an* office, *an* orange, *an* hour, *an* heir, *an* honest man

But we say :

a European, ***a*** university, ***a*** union

because these words begin with a consonant sound.

A boy met ***a*** man with ***an*** elephant. ***The*** boy saw ***the*** man feed *the* elephant.

A man once sailed on *a* ship to ***an*** island. ***The*** people of ***the*** island saw ***the*** man come off ***the*** ship.

A traveller followed ***a*** path through ***a*** forest and came to ***a*** bridge over ***a*** river. He crossed ***the*** bridge over ***the*** river and was glad to leave ***the*** path through ***the*** forest behind him.

It will be seen that when we speak about a thing for the first time we generally use *a* (or *an*).

When we speak about the same thing again we generally use **the**.

When we speak about a person or thing for the first time, it is not clear which one we mean. When we refer to the same person or thing again, it is clear which one we mean.

As a general rule, we use *the* when it is clear from the context which person or thing we mean; we use *a/ an* when it is not clear which one we mean.

Study the following examples :

The postman is coming. (We know which postman.)

A postman fell off his bicycle. (We don't know which postman. A postman = a certain postman)

Let's go to *the* park. (= the park we usually go to)

There is **a** park near Ideal School. (It is not clear which park is meant.)

The is used before superlative adjectives (e.g. best, tallest) and adjectives like *first, second, third,* etc.

Radha is *the cleverest* girl in the class.

Jawaharlal Nehru was *the* first Prime Minister of India.

No article is used before Abstract nouns, and nouns of material with a general meaning; as,

Honesty is the best policy.

Gold is more precious than *silver.*

No article is used in certain phrases consisting of a transitive verb followed by its object; as,

He took *offence.*

His clothes caught *fire.*

The enemies laid *siege* to the town.

No article is used in certain phrases consisting of a preposition followed by its object; as,

At home, at school, by day, by night, by land, by water, in hand, in bed, on horseback, on foot.

The is used before Common nouns which are names of things unique of their kind (that is, of which there is only one thing), *e.g.,*

The sun, *the* moon, *the* sky, *the* earth.

The is used before Common nouns when the name of an animal, plant, or other thing, is taken as a type of its class; as,

The cow is a useful animal.

The ostrich is a huge bird.

The banyan is a kind of fig tree.
[Do not say, "a kind of a fig tree." This is a common error.]

The is used with adjectives which do the work of nouns; as,
The poor are often happier than *the* rich.
Honour *the* brave, feed *the* hungry, clothe *the* naked, care for
the fatherless.

Note : *Do not forget that there are many exceptions to the above-mentioned rules.*

EXERCISE 1

Fill in the blank spaces with *a* or *an* or *the,* as may be suitable:

1. He looks as stupid as .... owl.

2. .... peacock is .... national bird of India.

3. The guide knows .... way.

4. Honest men speak .... truth.

5. Copper is .... useful metal.

6. He is .... honour to his country.

7. The children found .... egg in the nest.

8. French is .... easy language.

9. .... sun shines brightly.

10. English is .... language of .... people of England.

11. He is .... untidy boy.

12. I have come without .... umbrella.

13. .... lion is .... king of beasts.

14. Sri Lanka is .... island.

15. Varanasi is .... holy city.

16. Aladdin had .... wonderful lamp.

17. He returned after .... hour.

18. .... school will shortly close for Diwali holidays.

19. When did you buy .... calculator?

20. I first met him .... year ago.

21. .... Ganga is .... sacred river.

22. Which is .... longest river in India ?

Exchange your answers with another student, and discuss the mistakes if any.

EXERCISE 2

A. Insert *Articles* where necessary:

1. I have not seen him since he was child.

2. Umbrella is of no avail against thunderstorm.

3. How blue sky looks !

4. The doctor says it is hopeless case.

5. Get kilo of sugar from nearest grocer.

6. My favourite flower is rose.

7. What kind of bird is that ?

8. There is nothing like staying at home for comfort.

9. Moon did not rise till after ten.

10. Wild animals suffer when kept in captivity.

11. You must take care of your health.

12. Set back clock; it is hour too fast.

13. The poor woman has not rupee

14. Sun rises in east.

B. Read out your answers to each other in pairs or groups and discuss the mistakes if any.

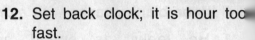
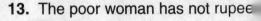

We use *a/ an* (apart from its use referred to before)

1. in the sense of "one"

   Please wait *a* minute.

2. to say what kind of thing or person something or somebody is, or somebody's job is

This is *a* useful book.

My aunt is *a* doctor.

Most proper nouns do not have an article. A few take *the*. They include the names of oceans (e.g. *the* Pacific), seas (e.g. *the* Black Sea), rivers (e.g. *the* Ganga), mountain groups (e.g. *the* Himalayas) and island groups (e.g. *the* West Indies).

24 Forms of the Personal Pronouns

Examine the *Pronouns* in italics in the following sentences:

1. *I* know Hari.
2. Hari knows *me*.
3. Hari is *my* cousin.
4. The pen he is using is *mine*.

I, me, my, mine. — These Pronouns refer to the person *speaking*, called the *first person*. They are therefore said to be of the first person, singular number.

Now examine the *Pronouns* in italics in the following sentences:

1. *We* love the child.
2. The child loves *us*.

3. He is *our* child.
4. Yes, he is *ours*.

We, us, our, ours. — These Pronouns refer to the person *speaking* and others for whom he (or she) speaks. They are of the first person, plural number.

You observe that Personal Pronouns of the First Person *change their form according to their Number and Case.*

	Singular	**Plural**
Nominative :	I	we
Possessive :	my, mine	our, ours
Objective :	me	us

EXERCISE 1

In the following sentences fill each blank with *I* or *me* :

1. You know that as well as ....
2. Between you and ...., it is not true.
3. Did you ask Abdul or .... ?
4. They blamed him and ....
5. Sohrab and .... went to the party.
6. I bought this bicycle for ...., not for you.
7. Will you let Hari and .... go to the cinema ?
8. Now we shall see who is the better man, you or ....

EXERCISE 2

In the following sentences fill each blank with *we* **or** *us* :

1. Have they done better than .... ?
2. .... boys were there.
3. They have deserved punishment as well as ....

Examine the *Pronouns* **in italics in the following sentences:**

1. *You* are late, Rama.
2. I shall punish *you.*
3. Where are *your* books ?
4. Are these books *yours* ?

    You, your, yours. — These Pronouns refer to the person *spoken to* called the *second person.* They are therefore said to be of the second person, singular number.

Now examine the *Pronouns* **in italics in the following sentences:**

1. *You* are late, boys.
2. I shall punish *you* all.
3. Where are *your* books ?
4. Are these books *yours* ?

    You observe that *you, your,* and *yours* are used for both singular and plural. Hence Personal Pronouns of the Second Person *change their form according to their Case.*

Singular and Plural	
Nominative :	you
Possessive :	your, yours
Objective :	you

    Notice that *you* is the common form for both numbers, in both the nominative and objective cases.

> **Note 1:** Even when only one person is spoken to or addressed, the Pronoun *you* takes a plural verb; as,
> You *are* mistaken, my boy.

> **Note 2:** In poetry, and sometimes in elevated prose, for the second person singular, *thou, thy, thine* and *thee,* according to the case, were used in older English ; as,
> I see *thee* daily weaker grow.
> We praise *Thee,* O God !
> *Thou* shalt not steal.

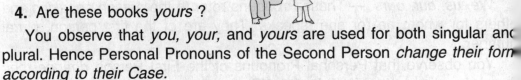

New Simple English Gramma

Examine the *Pronouns* in italics in the following sentences:

1. *He* is ill. I know *his* parents. I often go to see *him*. This book is *his*.

2. *She* is ill. I know *her* parents. I often go to see *her*. This book is *hers*.

3. *It* is of no use. *Its* handle is gone. Throw *it* away.

4. *They* have just arrived. *Their* father asked *them* to come. *They* have brought *their* books. These books are all *theirs*.

1. *He, his, him.* — These Pronouns refer to the person *spoken of,* called the *third person.* They are therefore said to be of the third person, singular number. They are used when the person spoken of is a male. Hence they are of the third person, masculine gender, singular number.

2. *She, her, hers.* — These Pronouns also refer to the person *spoken of.* But they are used when the person spoken of is a female. Hence they are of the third person, feminine gender, singular number.

3. *It, its.* — These Pronouns refer to the thing *spoken of.* Hence they are of the third person, neuter gender, singular number.

4. *They, their, theirs, them.* — These Pronouns refer to the persons (or things) *spoken of.* Hence they are of the third person, common gender, plural number.

You observe that Personal Pronouns of the third Person *change their form according to their Gender, Number, and Case.*

	SINGULAR		PLURAL	
	Mas.	*Fem.*	*Neu.*	*All Genders*
Nominative :	he	she	it	they
Possessive :	his	her, hers	its	their, theirs
Objective :	him	her	it	them

Note:

1. Remember to use the nominative form of the pronoun when used as the subject of a sentence, and the objective form when used as the object of a transitive verb or preposition.

2. In modern English, the objective case is used after the verb *be* . "Who is that ?" "It is *me*."

3. The objective case is used after *than* and *as* in comparisons.
   I am taller than *him.*
   He is not as tall as *me.*

EXERCISE 3

In the following sentences fill each blank with *he* or *him*:

1. They sent for you and ....
2. I am older than ....
3. John can speak French, as well as ....
4. We want you and .... to go.
5. Who is whispering ? It is ....
6. Are you sure it was not .... ?
7. He is so changed that I hardly knew it to be ....
8. I can play much better than ....

EXERCISE 4

In the following sentences fill each blank with *they* or *them* :

1. Pupils such as .... deserve to succeed.
2. Tell .... to go away.
3. Few did as well as ....
4. Can it be .... who are calling ?
5. How do you know .... are Italians ?

We have seen that each of the pronouns, except *he* and *it*, has two possessive forms.

The forms, *my, her, our, your, their,* are used only when preceding the noun they qualify; as,

This is *my* pen.

These are *our* books.

That is *your* book.

They are usually known as **Possessive Adjectives**.

The forms, *mine, hers, ours, yours, theirs*, are commonly used after the noun; as,

The dog *is mine.* That book is *yours.*

That dog of *mine* cost me two hundred rupees.

A friend of *theirs* lives in our neighbourhood.

EXERCISE 5

Suppose Rama is speaking to Hari, substitute the *Proper Pronouns* for their names in the following sentences:

1. Is this book Hari's ?
2. Did Rama hurt Hari ?
3. Hari can help Rama.
4. Rama should see Hari again tomorrow.
5. That pen is Rama's, not Hari's.

A pronoun must agree in number and gender with the noun for which it stands. That is, it should be of the same number and gender.

The *boy* passed because *he* worked hard.

The *girl* passed because *she* worked hard.

The *boys* and *girls* passed because *they* worked hard.

The *egg* broke because *it* fell on the floor.

The *eggs* broke because *they* fell on the floor.

As the *man* approached, I saw *him* clearly.

As the *woman* approached, I saw *her* clearly.

As we approached the *rock,* I saw *it* clearly.

As the *children* approached, I saw *them* clearly.

EXERCISE 6

Write *Pronouns* in agreement with their nouns in the following sentences:

1. The fowl ate the grain which .... had found.

2. The dog was hungry, so I fed ....

3. The moon gives no light as clouds cover ....

4. He spoke to Rama and Sita when he met ....

5. The bird can fly because .... has wings.

6. I looked for the book, but could not find ....

7. When the dog barked at Kashi, ... ran as fast as .... could.

8. I have five flowers; .... are all pink.

9. Abdul met Ali; .... talked for an hour.

10. The dog barked at Jane and ran after ....

11. I met Hari and Pandu. I took a walk with ....

12. Sita's brother gave .... a pearl necklace.

13. Sita has a pet dog; .... likes to play with ....

EXERCISE 7

Change the *Pronouns* as shown and make any other necessary changes:

1. Where are you going ? [she]
   [Where is she going ?]

2. I have a green parrot. [he]

3. He is yet a boy. [you]

4. He lost his parents in infancy. [I]

5. They groped their way in darkness. [we]

6. Are you speaking the truth ? [he]

7. He treats his children with great kindness. [they]

8. We like cricket better than football. [he]

9. I want some money. [she]

10. He has much money. [I]

11. You have done your lesson well. [he]

12. He was sleeping soundly. [we]

13. He spends his money foolishly. [she]

14. He has been shamefully treated [you]

15. Let us go out. [me]

16. He is going to Kolkata shortly [we]

17. Why are you late ? [he]

18. I blame myself for it. [we]

19. He has eaten nothing since yesterday. [they]

20. I am afraid of your dog. [she

21. He set himself a hard task [she]

22. They hid themselves. [he]

EXERCISE 8

Change the *Pronouns* in the following sentences and make any othe necessary changes :

1. We are very glad.
   [I am very glad.
   She is very glad.]

2. I live in Mumbai.

3. I fly my kite.

4. I have a gold watch.

5. I am going to Delhi.

6. I like a cold bath.

7. You speak in a very low voice.

8. She prepares her lessons carefully.

9. Did you see me from the window?

10. He is very rich, yet he is not happy.

11. He is at the top of his class.

12. I have some money in my pocket.

13. Are you not well ?

14. Don't you like to play ?

15. When do you read you lessons?

16. How far have we to go ?

17. Why does he sit idle ?

18. To whom are you talking ?

19. What have I got in my hand ?

20. Shall I go to the cinema, mother?

21. These books are mine.

22. We have mislaid our books and cannot find them.

23. She will not lend me her book.

Insert suitable *Pronouns* :

1. .... does his work carefully.

2. .... mends her own clothes.

3. .... still live in our old house.

4. .... weighs about a kilo.

5. .... is a kind and loving mother.

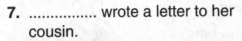

6. The books are where you left ....

7. .... wrote a letter to her cousin.

8. I think that .... have made a mistake.

9. My knife is sharper than ....

10. I congratulated .... on his good fortune.

11. Sita is absent, because .... is ill.

12. Here is your book; take .... away.

13. There were doors all round the hall, but .... were all locked.

14. " .... are not attending," said the Mouse to Alice severely.

15. The boys went into the garden, where .... saw a snake.

16. All her friends laughed at ....

17. All his friends laughed at ....

18. I gave .... a rupee and he thanked ....

19. She gave .... a rupee and I thanked ....

20. .... am a boy. .... are a man. .... is a woman. .... are children.

21. Is this my pencil or .... ?

22. I believe him because .... is truthful.

23. I believe .... because she is truthful.

24. Is .... your sister or your cousin ?

25. I looked for my pen but I did not find ....

26. Mary will help you if you ask ....

27. Do not answer unless .... know.

28. Boys often think .... are stronger than their sisters.

29. "Will .... walk into my parlour?" said the spider to the fly.

30. "What am .... to do ?" asked the lad.

Chapter 25

Forms of the Relative Pronouns

Examine the following sentences :

1. This is the boy *who* won the race.
2. This is the girl *who* is top of the class.
3. These are the people *who* wish to see you.
4. This is the boy *whom* I know.
5. This is the girl *whom* they saw.
6. These are the people *whom* we visited.
7. This is the man *whose* son is here.
8. This is the lady *whose* daughter is here.

9. These are the people *whose* children are here.

We see that the Relative Pronoun *who* has *different forms* for Objective and Possessive.

The forms are, however, the same for singular and plural, masculine and feminine.

Nominative :	who
Objective :	whom
Possessive :	whose

Examine the following sentences :

1. The tree *which* fell has been removed.
2. The trees *which* fell have been removed.
3. That is the book *which* I lost.
4. Those are the books *which* I lost.

In sentences 1 and 2 the Relative Pronoun *which* is in the nominative case; in sentences 3 and 4, in the *objective* case.

We therefore see that the **Relative Pronoun** *which* has the same form for the Nominative and Objective cases. It has also the same form in the singular and plural.

New Simple English Grammar

Note: The Relative Pronoun *which* has no Possessive case, but *whose* is sometimes used as a substitute for "of which"; as,

A triangle *whose* three sides are equal is called an equilateral triangle.

Examine the following sentences :

1. He *that* is content is rich.

2. Take anything *that* you like.

In the first sentence the Relative Pronoun *that* is in the *nominative* case, in the second, in the *objective* case.

We therefore see that the Relative Pronoun *that* has the same form for the Nominative and Objective cases. It has also the same form in the singular and plural.

Note: The Relative Pronoun *that* has no Possessive case and it is never used with a preposition preceding; as,

This is the boy *that* I told you *about.*

I know the house *that* he lives *in.*

Examine the following sentences :

1. *What* has happened is not clear.

2. I know *what* you want.

The Relative Pronoun *what* is used only in the *singular,* and has the same form in the Nominative and Objective.

Chapter 26

Use of the Relative Pronouns

As a general rule, the Relative Pronoun *who* is used for *persons* only. It may refer to a singular or a plural noun or pronoun.

The *man who* is honest is trusted.

The *children who* were there were frightened.

He prayeth best *who* loveth best.

They never fail *who* persevere.

Note. The Relative Pronoun *who* is sometimes used in referring to animals.

The Relative Pronoun *which* is used for *things without life* and for *animals.* It may refer to a singular or a plural noun.

The *castle which* you see was built by Shivaji.

The *books which* help you most are those which make you think.

The *dog which* he recently bought is an Alsatian..

The Relative Pronoun *that* is used for *persons, animals,* and *things.*

This is the *boy that* I told you about.

The wisest *man that* ever lived made mistakes.

The *horse that* he had sold me was a Waler.

It is only *donkeys that* bray.

I know the *house that* he lives in.

He has lost the *watch that* was presented to him.

The Relative Pronoun *what* refers to *things* only. It is used when the antecedent is omitted, and is equivalent to *that which* (or *the thing which*).

That is *what* I want. I say *what* I mean.

What I have you are welcome to.

What I have written, I have written.

The Relative Pronoun is generally omitted when it would be in the objective case; as,

Is this the book ∧ you want ?

Come and see the car ∧ I have just bought.

I am monarch of all ∧ I survey.

The Relative Pronoun should be placed as near as possible to its antecedent.

The *boy who* won the first prize is the son of my old friend. Mr. Latif.

Notice that it would mean something quite different if we separate the Relative Pronoun from its antecedent and say:

The boy is the son of my old friend Mr. Latif who won the first prize.

As the Relative Pronoun refers to a noun or pronoun (called its Antecedent), it must be of the same *number* and *person* as its Antecedent.

[Remember that it is the verb that shows the number and person of the Relative Pronoun.]

The *boy who was* lazy was punished.

The *boys who were* lazy were punished.

I, who am your king, will lead you.

You, who are mighty, should be merciful.

He that is contented is happy.

The *flowers which grow* in this garden are not for sale.

EXERCISE 1

Pick out the *Relative Pronouns* in the following sentences, name their Antecedents, and give the Person, Number, Gender, and Case of each:

1. The cat killed the rat that ate the corn.
2. Bring me the letters which the postman left.
3. I hate children who are cruel.
4. You have not brought the book that I asked for.
5. This is the juggler whom we saw yesterday.
6. He that eats till he is sick must fast till he is well.

EXERCISE 2

Fill in the blanks with suitable *Relative Pronouns* :

1. God helps those .... help themselves.
2. Is this the way .... leads to the station ?
3. We saw the dog .... worried the cat.
4. He is a man .... you can trust.
5. Where is the knife .... I gave you ?

6. Do you know .... has happened ?
7. Time .... is lost is never found again.

New Simple English Grammar

77

8. I do not believe .... you say.

9. It is an ill-wind .... blows nobody good.

10. They always talk .... never think.

11. Listen to .... I say.

12. The man to .... I spoke is a well-known doctor.

13. I did not know that Mr Ranade, ... I met in Pune, was your brother.

14. Who .... has ever been to India has not seen Agra ?

15. The pen .... you gave me is a very good one.

16. Bring me the letters .... the postman left.

17. Here are the books .... I found.

18. This is the juggler .... we saw yesterday.

19. He .... does his best shall be raised.

20. I know .... you mean.

21. He gave away .... he did not need.

EXERCISE 3

Work with another student. Join together each of the following pairs of sentences by means of a *Relative Pronoun* :

1. The thief stole the watch. The thief was punished.

2. Coal is found in here. It is a very useful mineral.

3. That boy bowls very well. You see him there.

4. He is a rogue. No one trusts him.

5. The boy tells lies. He deserves to be punished.

6. We got into a bus. It was full of people.

7. Little Red Riding Hood went to visit her grandmother. Her grandmother was ill in bed.

8. I heard some news. The news astonished me.

9. The boy fell off his bicycle. He has hurt his leg.

10. Here is the doctor. The doctor cured me of malaria.

11. He does his best. He should be praised.

12. The man is honest. The man is trusted.

13. The man is deaf. You spoke to the man.

14. I have found the umbrella. I lost it.

15. The dog bit the burglar. The burglar had broken into the house.

16. The child is ill. I saw the child yesterday.

17. The boys clapped heartily. They were watching the match.

Chapter 27

Forms of the Interrogative Pronouns

Examine the following sentences :

1. *Who* shouted ? Hari.
2. *Who* is she ? She is Sita, my cousin.
3. *Who* are those two people ? They are Rama and Sita, my cousins.
4. *Whom* did you see ? I saw Rama.
5. *Whom* do you know in the town ? I know very many people.
6. About *whom* are you talking?
7. *Whose* is this bat ? It is Rama's.
8. *Whose* is that suitcase? It is Tom's.
9. *Whose* are those names ? They are the names of the winners.

We observe that the words in italics in the above sentences are Interrogative Pronouns.

We also observe that the Interrogative pronoun *who* has *different forms* for Objective and Possessive.

The forms are however the same for singular and plural, masculine and feminine.

Nominative :	who
Possessive :	whose
Objective :	whom

The Interrogative pronouns *who, whom* and *whose* are used for *people* only.

EXERCISE 1

Insert in each of the blanks the proper form of *Interrogative Pronoun*:

1. .... do you want to see ?
2. .... is that ?
3. .... called to see you ?
4. .... are you writing to ?

5. .... do you mean ?
6. .... do you think I am ?
7. .... was that speaking to you ?
8. With .... are you living ?

9. From .... do you come ?

10. To .... were you speaking?

11. .... broke this window ?

12. .... is this pen ?

Examine the following sentences :

1. *Which* of these boys is your friend ?

2. *Which* of these girls is your sister ?

3. *Which* of these books is yours?

4. *Which* is the cow you want to sell ?

In the above sentences we see the Interrogative pronoun *which* is used in the nominative and objective cases. It has the same unchanged form in both cases.

It will be observed that *which* is used for *persons, animals,* and *things.*

Examine the following sentences :

1. *What* is that ?

2. *What* is worrying you ?

3. *What* are their names ?

4. *What* do you want ?

5. *What* are they talking about ?

The Interrogative pronoun *what* is used for *things* only and, like *which,* has the same form in the nominative and objective.

When the words *which* and *what* are used along with nouns, they are Adjectives ; as,

Which book is yours ?

What noise is that ?

EXERCISE 2

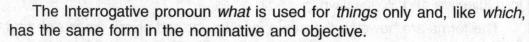

Fill up the blanks in the following sentences by using *who, whose, whom, which,* or *what* :

1. .... is singing ?

2. .... is your address ?

3. .... friend are you ?

4. .... do you want ?

5. .... have you got in your hand ?

6. .... was sitting by you ?

7. .... school does your brother attend ?

8. .... has taken my pencil ?

9. .... did you eat yesterday ?

10. To .... have you lent your book ?

11. In .... village do you live ?

12. By .... order did you enter the class ?

13. With .... will you go home?

14. By .... way did you come?

15. .... is this chair made of ?

16. Near .... desk were you standing ?

17. For .... did your father buy this cap ?

18. .... of these three pictures do you like the best ?

Note : Today *who* is used very often instead of *whom* in spoken English. *Whom* is used in a formal style. When *who* is used as the object of a preposition, the preposition comes at the end of the sentence. So sentences 4,5 and 6 on page 79 would be :

Who did you see ?

Who do you know in the town ?

Who are you talking about ?

EXERCISE 3

Now look at your answers to Exercises 1 and 2. Rewrite all the *whom*-questions using *who* and read them aloud.

Read these sentences :

1. He is *playing* cricket.
2. He *played* cricket.
3. He *was playing* cricket.
4. He *will play* cricket.

The same verb (*play*) is used in these sentences. But we find different forms of the verb in the sentences. The form in the first sentence (*is playing*) shows the present time. The forms in sentences 2 and 3 (*played* and *was playing*) show the past time. The form *played* refers to a completed action, while the form *was playing* refers to an action which was incomplete and was going on at a certain time in the past. The form *will play* in the last sentence shows the future time. Verb forms like these are called **Tenses**.

The tenses used in the above sentences are : Presesnt Continuous, Simple Past, Past Continuous and Simple Future. The forms of these and other commoner tenses are given at the end of this chapter.

When we talk about the grammar of verbs, we often use these terms : "base form" or "infinitive", "present participle" (*-ing* form), " past tense" and "past participle".

sing	- base form or infinitive without *to* (He can *sing* well.)
to sing	- infinitive with *to* (He would like *to sing*.)
singing	- present participle (He is *singing*.)
sang	- past tense (He *sang*.)
sung	- past participle (He has *sung*.),

In most English verbs the past tense and the past participle are the same. They are formed by adding *-ed* (or-*d*) to the base form, e.g.

talk	–	talked	clean	–	cleaned
work	–	worked	like	–	liked

Such verbs are called " regular verbs".

Other verbs are called "irregular". They make their past tense and past participle by a change of vowel or consonant or by a change of both, e.g.

Base form	Past tense	Past participle
ring	rang	rung
build	built	built

write	wrote	written
keep	kept	kept
bring	brought	brought

A few verbs, like *put, cut, shut, hit, cost,* have only one form.

Put the newspaper on the table. (base form)

I *put* the newspaper on the table at 7.30 after reading it. (past tense)

I have *put* the newspaper on the table. (past participle)

In old grammars, irregular verbs were called "strong verbs" and regular verbs were called "weak verbs".

Note the forms of the following tenses. The next chapters deal with the uses of these tenses.

Simple Presesnt Tense	Present Continuous Tense
I write.	I am writing.
You write.	You are writing.
He/She writes.	He/She is writing.
We write.	We are writing.
They write.	They are writing.
Simple Past Tense	**Past Continuous Tense**
I wrote.	I was writing.
You wrote.	You were writing.
He/ She wrote.	He/She was writing.
We wrote.	We were writing.
They wrote.	They were writing.
Present Perfect Tense	**Present Perfect Continuous Tense**
I have written.	I have been writing.
You have written.	You have been writing.
He/She has written.	He/She has been writing.
We have written.	We have been writing.
They have written.	They have been writing.

Simple Future Tense
I will/shall write.
You will write.
He/She will write.
We will/shall write.
They will write.

Note : "I/We *will*" is more usual than "I/We *shall*".

Chapter 29

Simple Present & Present Continuous Tense

We use the Simple Present Tense

1. for things that happen again and again
   I *go* for a walk every morning.
   He usually *reads* till midnight.
   She *waters* the plants daily.
   We often *listen* to the cassettes.

2. for general truths (= things that are always true)
   The earth *moves* round the sun.
   Rain *falls* from the clouds.
   The sun *shines* during the day.

3. for things that stay the same for a long time
   This watch *keeps* good time.
   They *live* in Chennai.
   Suresh *writes* nealty.
   Miss James *teaches* maths at Don Bosco school.

The Simple Present can also be used for the future. We use it when we talk about timetable.

The train *arrives* at 8.40.
Our school *opens* on 1st July.

EXERCISE 1

Complete the sentences using these verbs in the *Simple Present Tense*.

live fly eat shine do leave

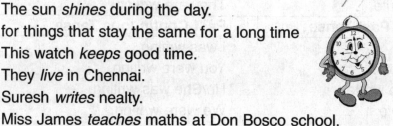

1. The stars .... at night.
2. Birds .... with their wings.
3. Fish .... in water.
4. The plane .... at 6.15.
5. Cows .... grass.
6. Tom .... his homework regularly.

What do you do every day ? Write six sentences using the *Simple Present Tense*.

Examples :

I get up at 6.00 every day.

I have breakfast at 7.30.

We use the Present Continuous Tense to talk about things which are happening now.

Anil *is doing* his homework (now).

Look : It *is raining*.

We *are learning* the uses of tenses.

The phone *is ringing*. Can you answer it ?

The Present Continuous is also used for things that people have planned or aranged to do in the future.

We *are going* to Darjeeling next Sunday.

I *am playing* tennis tomorrow.

They *are having* a party next week.

Look at the pictures below and describe what the people are doing. Begin each sentence with *He/She/They* and use the *Present Continuous Tense*. Number 1 has been done for you.

1.   He is picking a flower (or: flowers).

2.   3.   4.   5.

6.   7.   8.   9.

30

Simple Past & Past Continuous Tense

We use the Simple Past Tense for an action completed at some time in the past. We talk or think about a definite time in the past (e.g. yesterday, at 7.30 , last Monday, last month, in 2003).

I *saw* the movie last Sunday.

Sachin *scored* a century in the last match.

We *visited* Qutab Minar in 2002.

I *bought* this camera in Bangalore.

This tense is often used to tell a story.

EXERCISE 1

Below is a story that you already know. Fill in the blanks with the verbs in the box. Use the *Simple Past Tense*.

be drop see pick fly drink rise

A thirsty crow was flying around in search of water. It .... a pot near a house. There .... some water at the bottom of the pot. The crow's beak did not reach the bottom. It .... up some small stones and .... them one by one into the pot. Then the water............ and was near the top of the pot. The crow .... the water and .... away.

We use the Past Continuous Tense for an action which was in the middle of happening at a particular time in the past.

" What *were* you *doing* at 5.30 yesterday ?" "I *was playing* chess."

We *were watching* TV when Anil called.

It *was raining* when I came out.

As in the last two examples above, the Past Coutinuous is often used with the Simple Past. It shows that the action was continuing at a time when a new shorter action happened. The Simple Past is used for the new action.

EXERCISE 2

What were you doing at these times last Sunday ? Give true answers.

(1) 6 a.m.　　　(2) 10 a.m.　　　(3) 1.30 p.m.

(4) 4 p.m.　　　(5) 7 p.m.　　　(6) 10.30 p.m.

EXERCISE 3

Put the verbs in brackets into the *Simple Past* or *Past Continuous*. (You have to use both the tenses in each sentence.)

1. The boy (fall) when he (run).

2. I (have) a bath when the phone (ring).

3. Anita (burn) her hand while she (cook).

4. Usha (drop) her purse while she (get) into the car.

5. While I (work) in the garden, I (hurt) my back.

Chapter 31 — Present Perfect & Present Perfect Continuous Tense

We use the Present Perfect Tense for actions in the past when we are not thinking or talking about the exact time that they happened. There mey be results now. Sentences with the Present Perfect Tense connect the past and the present in some way.

I *have cleaned* the bike. (= The bike is clean now.)

Somebody *has broken* the window. (= The window is now broken.)

The school bus *has come* (= It is now here.)

I *have finished* my homework. (= I am free now)

Compare the above sentence with this :

I *finished* my homework an hour ago.

The Simple Past Tense is used in this sentence because we have mentioned the time that the action happened.

Use the Simple Past Tense, not the Present Perfect Tense, with words or phrases of past time which say when something happened.

Wrong : I *have met* Ramesh yesterday.

Right : I *met* Ramesh yesterday.

We can use the Present Perfect of verbs like *know, live, stay, work, be* for actions (or states) which began in the past and are still going on.

I *have known* him for a long time.

We *have lived* in Delhi since 1995.

Note that *for* is used with a length of time (e.g. *for* three days, *for* five years) and *since* is used with a point of time (e.g. *since* 8 o'clock, *since* Monday, *since* 2001).

The Present Perfect is often used with *ever* (in questions), *never, yet, already, once, twice, three times,* etc.

Have you ever *seen* a gorilla ?

I *have* never *visited* the Taj Mahal.

He *hasn't come* yet.

I *have* already *finished* the work.

I *have been* to America twice.

Complete the sentences using these verbs in the *Present Perfect Tense*.

repair pay close live cut cook

1. We ..... in Hyderabad for over ten years.
2. I ...... the phone bill.
3. I ...... the computer. You can use it.

4. She .... the dinner.
5. It is very cold, so I ...... the window.
6. Oh dear! I .... my finger.

EXERCISE 2

A. Pair-work

Make questions from this table. Take turns to ask and answer the questions.

Have you ever	seen travelled been to	by plane ? a tiger ? a zoo ? a circus ? the Taj Mahal ?

Example

Student A   :   Have you ever seen the Taj Mahal ?

Student B   :   No, I have never seen it./ Yes, I have seen it once/ twice/ several times.

We use the Present Perfect Continuous Tense to talk about actions which began at some time in the past and are still going on. This tense is often used with *How long, since* .... and for ....

The children *have been playing* since 4.30.

It *has been raining* for an hour.

How long have you *been waiting* ?

She *has been working* in this school for about six years.

For such actions we can use either the Present Perfect or the Present Perfect Continuous with verbs like *work, live, stay, lie,* etc. For example, there is almost no difference in meaning between the last sentence above and the following sentence :

She *has worked* in this school for about six years.

Don't use the Present Continuous Tense with *How long, since ......* and *for ....* .

Wrong   : I **am reading** since 7.30.

Right   : I **have been reading** since 7.30.

B. Fill in the blanks with the verbs in the box. Use the *Present Perfect Continuous*.

| listen watch learn play paint water |

1. They .... tennis since four o'clock.

2. He .... TV for over an hour.

3. Rupa and Rekha .... to the cassettes since 9.30.

4. He .... the plants since 6 o'clock.

5. I ...... French since last month.

6. He .... the gate for about two hours.

Chapter 32 — Simple Future Tense and "Going to" Form

We use the Simple Future Tense to talk about what we think or know will happen in the future.

I *will be* thirteen next Friday.

Perhaps he *will arrive* in time for lunch.

You *will find* a signpost at the end of the road.

I'm sure that you *will like* him.

I think she *will get* the job.

We also use the Simple Future Tense when we decide to do something at the time of speaking.

It is cold. I *will shut* the window.   OK, we *will come* tomorrow.

We use the *going to* form (= am/ is/ are + going to + base form), not the Simple Future Tense, to talk about things that we have already decided to do.

"Why are you filling the bucket with water ?" "I *am going* to wash the car."

We also use the *going to* form when there is something in the present which tells us about the future.

The clouds are very black. It *is going to* rain.

Look out ! That ladder *is going* to fall:

As you have learnt before, the Simple Present Tense and the Present Continuous Tense are also used to talk about the future. We use the Simple Present when we talk about timetables. The Present Continuous is used to talk about future plans.

EXERCISE 1

The verbs in the following sentences are in the Simple Past Tense. Change the sentences using the *Simple Future Tense* and expressions like "tomorrow", "tonight" "next week", etc.

Example

I *met* Mr Pratap Singh yesterday.

I *will meet* Mr Pratap Singh tomorrow.

1. I cleaned the motorbike yesterday.
2. We watched the video last night.
3. I phoned Mr Mehta last Sunday.
4. I bought some cassettes last week.
5. We were very busy yesterday evening. (...... this evening)
6. We played hockey yesterday afternoon.

EXERCISE 2

Look at the sentences you have written in the above exercise. Rewrite the sentences, using *going to*.

Chapter 33

Revision of Tense
(Exercises

EXERCISE 1

Choose the correct *Verb Form* to fill in each blank :

1. I ...... Anand an hour ago. (have seen/ saw)

2. This shop ..... on Fridays. (closes/ is closing)

3. I ...... at the bus stop at that time. (was/ am)

4. Look! The taxi .... (came/ has come)

5. Listen! Somebody .... at the door. (is tapping/ taps)

6. Mohan called when we .... lunch. (are having/ were having

7. "Why do you want to sell you car ?" "I ..... buy a car. (will buy am going to buy)

8. The moon ..... at night. (shine is shining)

9. Oh lovely! The moon ...... now (shines/ is shining)

10. He fell asleep while he ...... TV (was watching/ watched)

EXERCISE 2

A. Correct the following sentences :

1. I have phoned Suresh yesterday.

2. We are going to Delhi in the summer holidays every year.

3. I know him for a long time.

4. How long are you wearing glases ?

5. I am having a bath when the doorbell rang.

6. He is sleeping since 2 o'clock.

7. Mother Teresa has won the Nobel Prize in 1979.

8. Listen! Somebody cries.

9. He has gone out a few minutes ago.

10. According to the timetable, the next bus will go at 5.15.

B. Group Work

Read your answers to each other in groups of three and decide which answers are correct.

New Simple English Gramma

Chapter 34

Auxiliary and Modal Verbs

Auxiliary Verbs (or **Auxiliaries**) are "helping verbs" used with other verbs to form tenses, passive voice, questions, negatives, etc. or to express meanings like ability, permission, possibility and necessity. Here is a list of auxiliaries :

> be (am/ is/ was, etc) have (have / has / had) do (do / does / did) can could may might will would shall should must ought

Need and *dare* are sometimes used as auxiliaries.

Auxiliaries come before the subject in questions and can be put before *not*.

She is busy.
{ *Is* she busy ?
She *is* not busy.

They have arrived.
{ *Has* he arrived ?
He *has* not arrived.

He can drive.
{ *Can* he drive ?
He *cannot* drive.

She should go.
{ *Should* she go ?
She *should* not go.

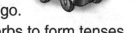

The auxiliaries *be* and *have* are used with ordinary verbs to form tenses.

He *is* dancing. (Present Continuous Tense)

They *have* videoed the programme. (Present Perfect Tense)

The auxiliary *be* is also used to make passive forms.

Cheese *is* made from milk.

The programme *was* videoed.

The auxiliary *do* is used to form questions and negatives in the Simple Present and Simple Past tenses.

She acts on TV.
{ *Does* she act on TV ?
She *does* not act on TV.

India won.
{ *Did* India win ?
India *did* not win.

> The auxiliaries *can, could, may, might, will, would, shall, should, must*, and *ought* (sometimes *need* and *dare*) are called **Modal Verbs** or **Modals/ Modal Auxiliaries**.

After modal verbs we use the base form of ordinary verbs. *Ought* is an exception. We use *ought* with the *to*-infinitive (e.g. You ought to go.)

We often use modal verbs to talk about ability, permission, necessity, etc. Each modal verb has more than one use.

Modal	Use	Examples
can	1. ability	He *can* speak five languages.
	2. permission	*Can* I use your phone ?
		You *can* go now.
	3. request	*Can* I have a glass of water, please ?
		Can you get me a ticket ?
	4. offer	*Can* I help you ?
could	1. ability (past)	I *could* swim when I was seven.
	2. request	*Could* you get me a ticket ? (more polite than *can*)
may	1. permission	You *may* use my computer.
		May I come in ?
	2. possibility	He *may* come today.
might	1. permission	You *might* go now.
	2. possibility	He *might* come today. (less sure than *may*)
will	1. future action	Perhaps it *will* rain tonight.
	2. request	*Will* you give me a lift ?
	3. offer	*Will* you have some tea ?
would	1. request	*Would* you lend me your camera ?
	2. offer	*Would* you like a cup of coffee ?
shall	1. future action	I *shall* see him tomorrow.
	2. offer	*Shall* I carry the bag for you ?
	3. suggestion	*Shall* we go to the beach ?
should	necessity	You *should* apply for the job.
must	1. necessity	I *must* get up at five tomorrow.
	2. certainty	She *must* be at home now.
ought	necessity	You *ought* to obey your parents.

Match the sentences on the left with the uses of the *modals* on the right.

1. I *must* make a phone call.

2. She has walked a long way : she *must* be tired.

3. *Will* you close the window, please ?

4. We *will* be away next weekend.

5. She c*an* speak French fluently.

6. *Shall* I get a taxi for you ?

7. *Shall* we go for a swim ?

8. *Can* I go out ?

9. She *may* arrive tomorrow.

(a) certainty

(b) ability

(c) necessity

(d) permission

(e) request

(f) possibility

(g) future action

(h) suggestion

(i) offer

Examine the following sentences :
1. Rama *hits* the ball.
2. The ball *is hit* by Rama.

In the first sentence the verb (*hits*) shows that the subject (Rama) doe the action, or that the subject *acts*. The verb (*hits*) is therefore said to be i the **Active Voice**.

In the second sentence the verb (*is hit*) shows that the action is done t the subject (*ball*). The verb (*is hit*) is therefore said to be in the **Passive Voice**

When the verb shows that the subject *does* the action, the verb is said to be in the **Active Voice**.

When the verb shows that the subject *receives* or *suffers* the action, the verb is said to be in the **Passive Voice.**

[*Passive* means *receiving* or *suffering*.]

The object of the verb in the active voice becomes the subject of the ver in the passive voice.

The passive of a verb is made by adding a suitable form of *be* to the past participle ; as,

Active Voice	Passive Voice
take takes	am taken is taken are taken
took	was taken were taken
has taken have taken	has been taken have been taken
am taking is taking are taking	am being taken is being taken are being taken

was taking were taking	was being taken were being taken
will take can/ may/ must take	will be taken can/ may/ must be taken

xamples:

Active Voice	Passive Voice
1. Bees *make* honey.	Honey *is made* by bees.
2. The bird *built* a nest.	A nest *was built* by the bird.
3. Somebody *has stolen* her purse.	Her purse *has been stolen* (by somebody).
4. The mason *is building* the wall.	The wall *is being built* (by the mason).
5. Anil *was painting* the gate.	The gate *was being painted* by Anil.
6. I *will invite* the Joshis.	The Joshis will be invited (by me).
7. You *may return* the CD tomorrow.	The CD *may be returned* (by you) tomorrow.

As you must have noticed, in Sentences 3, 4, 6, and 7, the *by*-phrase (= by + doer of the action) is put in brackets. It would be better to omit the *by*-phrase in those sentences. We usually leave out the *by*-phrase if we do not know the doer or if it is not necessary to mention the doer.

EXERCISE 1

Pick out the Verbs in the following sentences, and tell whether they are in the *Active* or in the *Passive Voice* :

1. He is liked by all.
2. The boy made a kite.
3. The cat drank all the milk.
4. Little Bo-Peep has lost her sheep.
5. The cat was chased by the dog.
6. The sudden noise frightened the dog.
7. The letter was posted yesterday.
8. The thief was caught.
9. Hari is often helped by his brother.
10. A stone struck him on the head.
11. Some boys fly kites.
12. He is carrying a lot of luggage.

EXERCISE 2

Rewrite the following sentences using the *Passive Voice* of the verb:
1. The man cut down the tree.
2. The jackal followed the tiger.

New Simple English Grammar

97

3. His teacher praised him.
4. He made a very remarkable discovery.
5. He invited us into his house.
6. Shivaji defied the Mughal Emperor.
7. Ravi feeds the dog everyday.
8. The police have arrested him.
9. Your behaviour vexes me.
10. He scored fifty runs.
11. We expect good news.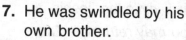
12. Everyone respects him.
13. They are repairing the bridge.
14. He was watching us.
15. The girl spilt the milk.
16. My cousin has drawn this picture.

EXERCISE 3

Rewrite the following sentences using the *Active Voice* of the verb:

1. America was discovered by Christopher Columbus.
2. He was treated ungratefully by his sailors.
3. The work must be done by you and your brother.
4. The match was won by the High School.
5. We will be blamed by everyone.
6. The first railway was built by George Stephenson.
7. He was swindled by his own brother.
8. The Prime Minister was welcomed by the people.
9. The child was knocked down by a car.
10. By whom was this jug broken ?
11. It was broken by me.

EXERCISE 4

In the following sentences change the *Voice*:

1. The peon opened the gate.
2. The boy was bitten by a dog.
3. The sudden noise frightened the horse.
4. He will finish the work in a fortnight.
5. The bird was killed by a cruel boy.
6. The dog chased the sheep.
7. A stone struck me on the head.
8. The trees were blown down by the wind.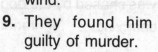
9. They found him guilty of murder.
10. By whom was this done ?

36

Mood

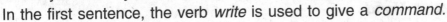

Examine the following sentences :

1. Boys! *Write* neatly.
2. I wish all boys *could* write neatly.
3. Only some boys *write* neatly.

In the first sentence, the verb *write* is used to give a *command*.

In the second sentence, the verb *could write* is used to express a *wish*.

In the third sentence, the verb *write* is used to state a *fact*.

Thus we see that the same verb *write* is used in three different ways or manners or modes, namely,

(1) to give a command,

(2) to express a wish, or

(3) to state a fact.

Anyone of these three different *manners* in which a verb may be used to express our thought is called its **Mood**.

When the verb *gives a command* or *makes an entreaty*, it is said to be in the **Imperative Mood**.

Open the door.

Go away !

Honour thy father and thy mother.

Excuse me.

Have pity on them.

In each of these sentences the verb is in the **Imperative Mood**.

Note: The subject of a verb in the Imperative Mood is usually not expressed but understood.

VERB EXPRESSES A MERE SUPPOSITION OR A WISH OR DOUBT.

I wish I were a millionaire

If we win the match....

When the verb *expresses a mere supposition* or *a wish* or *doubt* of any kind it is said to be in the **Subjunctive Mood**.

If I *were* you, I would not do it.
I wish I *had* a car.
I wish that he *would forgive* me.
Long *live* the Prime Minister !
God *bless* you !
Heaven *help* us !

In each of these sentences the verb in italics is said to be in the **Subjunctive Mood.**

When the verb *states a fact,* or *asks a question,* it is said to be in the **Indicative Mood**.

Rama *made* a hundred runs.
A hundred runs *were made* by Rama.
How many runs *did* Rama *make* ?

In each of these sentences the verb is in the **Indicative Mood.**

EXERCISE

Give the *Moods* of the verbs in the following sentences:

1. Take care of your health.
2. Perhaps it will rain tomorrow.
3. Give us this day our daily bread.
4. May you always be happy !
5. If I were king, you would be queen.
6. Mind your own business.
7. God bless you !
8. Turn the tap off.
9. I wish I could paint.

10. If he were here, he would help us.
11. Speak the truth.
12. I wish I were at home now.
13. Please come tomorrow.
14. I wish my father were here today.
15. Be good and you will be happy.
16. I wish I were older.
17. I shall not forgive him unless he asks my pardon.
18. If I were you, I would not go.

Chapter 37

The Infinitive

In this chapter and the next we shall consider certain words, which are Verb-Nouns. They are formed from verbs, and are partly like a noun and partly like a verb.

| To play | To sing | To dance | To read |

A Verb-Noun

Examine these sentences :

1. Rama likes to play cricket.
   [To play *what* ? Cricket.]
2. Rama likes to play daily.
   [To play *when* ? Daily.]

We notice that *to play* is formed from the verb *play*; it is therefore like a verb in some respects : for example, (i) it *may* take an object, and (ii) it *may* be qualified by an adverb.

In sentence 1, *to play*, like a transitive verb, takes the object *cricket*.

In sentence 2, *to play*, like a verb, is qualified by the adverb *daily*.

Now examine these sentences :

1. To play is his great delight.
2. He likes to play volleyball daily.

To play is the *name* of an action, the action of playing. *To play* is therefore like a noun : for example, (i) as in sentence 1, it *may* stand as the subject of a verb, or (ii) as in sentence 2, it *may* stand as the object of a verb.

We have seen before that *to play* is like a verb, and now we see that it is also like a noun. *To play* is therefore a Verb-Noun.

In Grammar, a Verb-Noun like *to play* is called an **Infinitive**.

Pick out the *Infinitive* in the following sentences and state whether each is used as subject or object of a verb :

1. Hari likes to ride.
2. He refused to obey his orders.
3. To play cricket is pleasant.
4. I like to swim.
5. He promised to help me.

6. He used to say so.
7. I hope to hear good news.
8. He tried to help his friend.
9. I wish to go home.
10. To speak the truth is your first duty.

The Infinitive is usually used with the word *to* before it, but sometimes it is found without *to*.

I bade him *go*.

We heard you *sing*.

I made him *run*.

I saw him *arrive*.

You need not *wait*.

Let him *sit* there.

I can *rid* your town of rats.

You may *go*.

He should *work*.

You must *work*.

Good bye! See You..

Examine the following sentences :

1. *To drive* a motor-car well requires skill.

2. *Driving* a motor-car well requires skill.

[*To drive* is formed from the verb *drive,* so it is like a verb. Being like a verb, it takes an object (*motor-car*), and is modified by an adverb (*well*).

To drive names an action, the action of driving; so it is like a noun also.

Being like a noun, it is used as the subject of a verb *(requires)*.

To drive is therefore a Verb-Noun.

[We shall now see that, like the Infinitive *to drive, driving* is also a Verb-Noun.]

Driving is formed from the verb *drive,* so it is like a verb.

Being like a verb, it takes an object (*motor-car*), and is modified by an adverb (*well*).

Driving names an action, the action of driving; so it is like a noun also.

Being like a noun, it is used as the subject of a verb (*requires*).

Driving is therefore a Verb-Noun.

In Grammar, a Verb-Noun (such as *driving*) which ends in *-ing* is called a **Gerund**.

Examine these sentences :

1. He likes *driving* a motor-car.

2. He is very careful in *driving* a motor-car.

It will be noticed that in sentence 1, the Gerund *driving* is the object of the verb *likes.*

In sentence 2 the Gerund *driving* is governed by the preposition *in.*

Note: The Gerund is most commonly governed by a preposition.

EXERCISE

Pick out the *Gerunds* in the following sentences, and state whether each is subject, object, or used after a preposition :

1. Do you like driving the car ?

2. He likes reading poetry.

3. Children love making mud castles.

4. Helping the poor is our great duty.

5. The miser hated spending money.

6. Hunting tigers is a favourite sport in this country.

7. Avoid catching cold.

8. Asking questions is easy.

9. He was punished for telling a lie.

10. The afternoon was spent in playing cards.

11. Be careful in driving the car.

12. He was afraid of telling the truth.

13. Bullocks are used for drawing carts.

14. He is fond of collecting stamps.

In this chapter we shall show that, just as we have Verb-Nouns, so we have a Verb-Adjective, that is, an adjective formed from a verb.

Examine these sentences :

1. That man is lazy.

    [Which boy ? *That* man.]

2. See Rama driving.

    [Which Rama ? Rama *driving.*]

That points out the man, and is therefore an Adjective.

Driving refers to (or points out) Rama, and is therefore like an adjective.

Now examine these sentences :

1. See Rama driving a car.

    [Driving *what* ? — A motor-car.]

2. See Rama driving skilfully.

    [Driving *how* ? — Skilfully.]

Driving is formed from the verb *drive;* it is therefore like a verb in some respects: for example, (i) it *may* take an object, and (ii) it *may* be qualified by an adverb.

In sentence 1, *driving,* like a transitive verb, takes the object *motor-car*.

In sentence 2, *driving,* like a verb, is qualified by the adverb *skilfully*.

We also see that *driving* refers to Rama, and is therefore like an adjective.

The word *driving* is therefore partly a verb and partly an adjective. In Grammar, a Verb-Adjective such as *driving,* is called a **Participle**.

EXERCISE 1

Pick out the *Participles* in the following sentences :

1. We saw a man leading a monkey.

2. I met him coming down the street.

3. Mounting his horse, the soldier rode away.

4. Clapping its hands for joy, the child laughed loudly.

5. I can hear him singing a song.

6. Singing in a chorus, we went on our way.

7. I pity that woman carrying such a heavy load on her head.

8. The boys, playing in the maidan, had a merry time.

9. Waving their handkerchiefs, the people cheered the President.

10. They heard the people ringing the bells.

Examine the words in *italics* :

The car, *driven* recklessly by Rama, dashed against a tree.

[*Which* car ? Driven *how* ?]

Driven is like an adjective. Why ?

Driven is also like a verb. Why ?

Driven is therefore a Verb-Adjective, *i.e.*, a Participle.

Examine the following sentences :

1. I saw Rama *driving a car.*

2. The car, *driven* recklessly by Rama, dashed against a tree.

When I saw Rama, he was driving a car; the action of driving was *going on* or was *incomplete* or *imperfect*. But when the motor-car dashed against a tree, the action of driving was *finished* or *complete* or *perfect*.

Driving expresses an *unfinished* action.

Driven expresses a *finished* action.

Participles ending in *-ing* describe *incomplete* actions, and are called **Present Participles.**

Participles ending in *-ed, -en, -d*, and *-t* describe *completed* actions, and are called **Past Participles.**

Further examples of Past Participles :

I saw a cord *stretched* across the road.

There were many trees *laden* with fruit.

The thieves, *caught* in the act, were severely punished.

EXERCISE 2

Pick out the *Present* and *Past Participles* in the following sentences and state the noun or pronoun to which each refers:

1. Walking along the road, he saw a cobra.

2. Hearing the noise, he looked through the window.

3. Deceived by his friends, he lost all hope.

4. Surrounded by the enemy, the army was forced to surrender.

5. Staggering back, he sank to the ground.

6. Landing at Calais, we proceeded to Paris.

7. Having no guide with us, we lost our way.

8. Driven by hunger, he stole a piece of bread.

9. I saw the boy posting the letter.

10. I saw the letter posted.

11. A soldier, wounded in the war, came limping by.

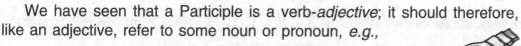

12. Taking pity on the mouse, the magician turned it into a cat.

13. He walked away whistling.

We have seen that a Participle is a verb-*adjective*; it should therefore, like an adjective, refer to some noun or pronoun, *e.g.,*

Walking along a road, a boy found a watch.

[Here the Participle *walking* refers to the noun *boy.*]

The following sentence is incorrect :

Walking along a road, a watch was found.

Here the Participle *walking* does not refer to the noun *watch*—the *watch* was not walking. Then who was walking? Obviously the noun or pronoun to which the participle *walking* should refer is not mentioned. The sentence is therefore incorrect. We should therefore rewrite it as :

Walking along a road, a person found a watch.

■ EXERCISE 3 ■

A. Examine each sentence and state whether it is *correct* or *incorrect*. If correct, point out the noun or pronoun to which the Participle refers. Rewrite correctly all incorrect sentences.

1. Wishing to borrow a book, he called on me yesterday.

2. Returning from the theatre, it began to rain.

3. Beaten at every point, the enemy fled from the field.

4. Running across the road, the child fell.

5. While cleaning the cage, the bird escaped.

6. Walking along the street, a hundred-rupee note was found.

7. Surrounded by the enemy, the battle was lost.

8. Standing on the top of the hill, the eye roams over a beautiful landscape.

B. Interact with two other students and revise your answers if necessary.

Examine these sentences :

1. Killing birds is a cruel sport.
2. I hate that boy killing birds.

In sentence 1, *killing* is a Gerund, and in sentence 2, *killing* is a Present Participle.

As the same word ending in *-ing* may be either a Gerund or a Present Participle, be very careful not to confuse the Gerund with the Present Participle.

EXERCISE 4

Pick out — (i) the *Gerunds*, (ii) the *Present Participles* :

1. I remember reading the book long ago.
2. Preparing the meal required only a short time.
3. I do not like working these sums.
4. I saw Mr Patel running for a bus.
5. Running for a bus, he slipped and fell.
6. The boys love swimming in the sea.
7. A great wave came rolling towards the boat.
8. We met a woman carrying a heavy load.
9. Feeling quite secure, the burglar slept soundly.
10. Hearing the noise, he ran to the window.
11. Jumping over the fence, the thief escaped.
12. Entering the room, I found the light quite dazzling.
13. Out of the houses the rats came tumbling.
14. I am tired of working these sums.
15. The boys are very fond of swimming in the sea.

Examine the words in *italics* :

Few can face a *roaring* lion.
[*Which* lion ? A *roaring* lion.]
A *barking* dog seldom bites.
Have you seen *falling* stars ?
A *burnt* child dreads the fire.
Beware of a *wounded* tiger.

In the above sentences, the Participles *roaring, barking*, etc., are used as Adjectives *in front of* nouns.

Chapter *40* — Number and Person

Examine these sentences :

1. The boy *plays.*
2. The boys *play.*

In the first sentence the subject, *boy,* is in the singular number; so the verb, *plays,* is also in the singular.

In the second sentence the subject, *boys,* is in the plural number; so the verb, *play,* is also in the plural.

Hence we say that a verb takes the same *number* as its subject.

Note: Though the verb takes the same number as its subject, it does not always change in form. For example, we say:

I play.   We play.   They play.

Examine these sentences :

1. I play.
2. He plays.

The subjects in both the sentences are in the singular number. But the subject in the first sentence is a pronoun of the *first* person, while the subject in the second sentence is a pronoun of the *third* person.

So we see that the verbs here change in form according to the *person* of their subjects.

Hence we say that a verb takes the same *person* as its subject.

Note: Verbs have three persons, and though a verb takes the same person as its subject, it does not always change in form. For example, we say:

I play.   You play.   They play.

We may now say that *the verb agrees with its subject in number and person;* that is, the verb must be of the same number and person as its subject.

EXERCISE 1

**Put *Verbs* in agreement with the subjects, in the following sentences.
Use the present tense :**

1. Cats .... mice.

2. This cat often .... mice.

3. The mouse .... in a hole.

4. He .... the truth.

5. I .... a little English.

6. The cow .... two horns.

7. Coconut trees .... very useful.

8. April .... thirty days.

9. My boots .... thick soles.

10. The books .... in the desk.

11. Government .... the law.

EXERCISE 2

Supply a *Subject* in agreement with each of the following predicates:

1. .... lives here.

2. .... live here.

3. .... are waiting for you.

4. .... study French.

5. .... takes too much liquor.

6. .... passes examinations easily.

7. .... fail frequently.

8. .... learns drawing.

VERB IN THE SAME NUMBER AND PERSON AS ITS SUBJECT

The girls dance

The girl dances

The Verb agrees with its Subject in Number and Person (Chapter 40). Thus we say —

The boy *plays.* The boys *play.*

I *play.* He *plays.* They *play.*

Special applications of the rule are given below.

Two or more singular subjects, joined by *and* take a verb in the plural; as,

Latif and Abdul *are* here.

Cotton and jute *grow* in India.

Hari, Rama and Govind *go* to the same school.

Rustum and Sohrab *were* Persian heroes.

He and his friend *have* arrived.

He and I *are* partners.

Note 1: If two singular nouns, joined by and, refer to the same person or thing, the verb is singular; as,

My cousin and friend has come.

Note 2: If two singular nouns, joined by and, express one idea, the verb is singular; as,

The horse and carriage is at the door.

Bread and milk is his only food.

Note 3: If two singular subjects are preceded by *each* or *every*, the verb is singular; as,

Every boy and girl *was* ready.

Each day and each hour *brings* its duty.

Two or more subjects in the singular joined by **either .... or** or **neither .....
nor**, take a verb in the singular; as,

Either Balu or Govind *is* there.

Either Hari or Karim *has* broken the jug.

Neither Rama nor Hari *was* there.

Neither he nor his brother *is* present.

Note 1: When two subjects, joined by *either ... or* or *neither ... nor,* are
of different numbers, the verb must be plural, and the plural subject must be
placed next the verb; as,

Either Rama or his brothers have done this.

Neither Sohrab nor his friends were hurt.

Note 2: When two subjects, joined by *either .... or* or *neither ... nor,* are
pronouns of different persons, the verb agrees with the pronoun nearer to it;
as,

Either he or I *am* mistaken.

Neither you nor he *is* to blame.

But it is better to say —

Either he *is* mistaken, or I *am.*

He *is* not to blame, nor *are* you.

When a noun in the singular number is joined to a second noun by *with,*
or *as well as*, the verb is singular; as,

The chief, with all his men, *was* killed.

Rama, as well as Hari, *likes* hot curry.

Some nouns, which are plural in form, but singular
in meaning, take a singular verb; as,

The news *is* true.

A collective noun takes a singular verb when the collection is thought of
as a whole; a plural verb when the *individuals* of which it is composed are
thought of; as,

The committee *was* unanimous.

The committee *were* divided in opinion.

The crew *was* large.

The crew *were* quarrelling among themselves.

There *are* a large number of boys in this class.

A number of boys *were* caught copying.

The mob *was* bent on mischief.

The mob *were* scattered by the police.

EXERCISE 1

In each of the following sentences supply a *Verb* in agreement with its Subject :

1. There .... six girls in the class.

2. Either Rustum or Sohran .... to be blamed.

3. Two and two .... four.

4. On his desk .... his book and pencil.

5. Neither he nor we .... wrong.

6. Here .... Abdul and Hamid.

7. A ring as well as a brooch .... been stolen.

8. Neither of them .... returned.

9. .... Rama or Arjun captain of the school ?

10. Neither bread nor rice .... bad for you.

11. Both bread and rice .... bad for you.

12. Ganpat with his friend .... come today.

13. Bread and butter .... better than bread or butter.

14. Forty yards............ a good distance.

15. Neither he nor she .... present yesterday.

16. Balu with Rama .... in the garden.

17. Balu and Rama .... in the garden.

18. The jury .... of twelve persons.

19. Each of the boys .... punished.

20. *The Arabian Nights* .... delighted many children.

21. Neither he nor I .... there that day.

22. Kindness as well as justice .... to be our guide.

23. Rama with three other boys .... caned.

24. *Gulliver's Travels* .... read by all pupils.

25. A good man and useful citizen .... passed away.

26. Seven hundred rupees .... the price of this camera.

$2 + 2 = 4$

27. The jury .... discharged.

28. The jury .... divided in their opinion.

29. Every boy and girl .... taught to read and write.

30. Fifty rupees .... too much for this article.

31. Both of you .... mistaken.

32. One of you .... mistaken.

33. There .... been many showers today.

34. Where .... all the people gone ?

EXERCISE 2

In each of the following sentences supply a *Verb* in agreement with its Subject:

1. A packet of sweets .... given to each child.

2. The mother of these poor children .... dead.

3. The mistakes of the child .... amusing.

4. Which of you two .... willing to go ?

5. He, with his father, ... among the first to arrive.

6. There .... several mistakes in your work.

7. *Tom Brown's School Days* .... interesting.

8. Milk and soda .... a refreshing drink.

9. One of the boys .... hurt in the tournament.

10. The ship with the entire crew .... lost.

11. Every one of your sums .... wrong.

12. Not one of the mangoes .... ripe.

13. Rats and mice .... much damage.

14. The difficulty of obtaining pure milk and *ghee* .... great.

15. Not one of you .... done the sum correctly.

16. Man's happiness or misery .... in a great measure in his own hands.

17. The spelling of some words Pneumonia .... difficult.

18. The quality of the mangoes .... very good.

19. Every one of them .... killed.

20. There .... many objections to such a plan.

Comparison of Adverbs

Some adverbs, like adjectives, have three degrees of comparison. Such adverbs are generally compared like adjectives.

If the adverb is of one syllable, we form the Comparative by adding *–er,* and the Superlative by adding *–est* to the Positive; as,

Positive	Comparative	Superlative
Hard	harder	hardest.
Long	longer	longest.
Soon	sooner	soonest.
Near	nearer	nearest.

Adverbs ending in *–ly* form the Comparative by adding *more* and the Superlative by adding *most;* as,

Positive	Comparative	Superlative
Neatly	more neatly	most neatly.
Swiftly	more swiftly	most swiftly.

The crow flies *swiftly.*

The hawk flies *more swiftly* than the crow.

Pigeons fly *most swiftly* of all birds.

But note : *early, earlier, earliest.*

I came early this morning.

Rama came *earlier.*

Hari came *earliest* of all.

A few adverbs are compared *irregularly :*

Positive	Comparative	Superlative
Well	better	best.
Badly	worse	worst.
Much	more	most.
Little	less	least.
Late	later	latest, last.
Far	farther	farthest.

Rama writes *well.*

Arjun writes *better* than Rama.

Hari writes *best* of all.

Rama Arjun Hari

Some adverbs cannot be compared, *e.g.,*

thus, now, then, here, there, once, twice, very, almost, half, not, consequently.

EXERCISE 1

Give the *three Degrees of Comparison* **of the following** *Adverbs*:

better, least, often, long, last, cleverly.

Formation of Adverbs: A great many adverbs are formed from adjectives by adding **-ly,** sometimes with a slight change; as,

kind, kindly; swift, swiftly; clever, cleverly; brave, bravely; nice, nicely; heavy, heavily; happy, happily; true, truly; noble, nobly.

EXERCISE 2

Form *Adverbs* **from the following adjectives, and use each one in a sentence:**

frequent, usual, careless, former, right, eager, easy, beautiful, wrong.

Form of Adverbs: Some adverbs have the *same form* as the corresponding adjectives; as,

Adverb	*Adjective*
It is raining *hard.*	This is a *hard* sum.
May you live *long !*	It is a *long* road.
I *little* expected this.	I have *little* money.
Come *early.*	Come by an *early* train.
Don't talk so *loud.*	He spoke in a *loud* voice.
Rama can bowl *fast.*	Rama is a *fast* bowler.

EXERCISE 3

Use the following words in sentences (1) as *Adverbs* **(2) as** *Adjectives*:

fast, next, much, near, quick, slow, right, only, enough.

An adverb which modifies an adjective or another adverb is always placed *immediately before* the word it modifies, *e.g.,*

The load is *very* heavy for a horse.

The child is *too* young for school.

Rama is a *rather* lazy boy.

You walk *too* quickly.

He struck the horse *most* cruelly.

He spoke *quite* angrily.

Do not speak *so* fast.

The adverb *enough* is the only exception to this rule, for it is always placed *after* the word which it modifies; as,

This is a house large *enough* for our purpose.

Speak loud *enough* to be heard.

There is no hard and fast rule as to the exact position of an adverb which modifies a verb in a simple sentence.

Note, however, that *an adverb should generally be placed as near as possible to the word which it modifies.*

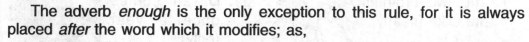

1. He walked *fast.*

2. He *never* spoke to any one.

3. He performed his duty *creditably.*

4. I feel this insult *keenly.*

[It will be noticed that when a verb is transitive with an object following, as in 3 and 4, the adverb usually *follows* the object.]

5. I could *easily* find it out.

6. I shall *certainly* miss him.

7. I have *seldom* seen such a thing.

8. I shall be *utterly* undone.

[It will be noticed that the adverb is usually placed *between* the auxiliary verb and the ordinary verb.]

When an adverb modifies a whole *sentence,* it is usually placed first in the sentence; as,

Fortunately, he was not hurt.

Unfortunately, he thinks too highly of himself.

Certainly, you are wrong.

The word *only* is frequently misplaced. It should be placed *immediately before* the word it modifies. Notice that the following four sentences have not the same meaning though the same words are used.

Only he lent me a book (*i.e., he* and nobody else).

He *only* lent me a book (*i.e.,* he *lent* it; he did not give it away).

He lent *only* me a book (*i.e.,* he lent a book to *me* and to nobody else).

He lent me *only* a book (*i.e.,* merely a *book,* and nothing else).

EXERCISE

Put the *Adverbs* into the following sentences so as to make sense:

1. The two brothers are alike (nearly).

2. He has promised to pay (faithfully).

3. There were three or four boys late (only).

4. I did not want to come (really).

5. I came to return a book (merely).

6. We can succeed by hard work (only).

7. We should speak ill of the dead (never).

8. He invited me to visit him (often).

9. I am determined to yield this point (never).

10. He charged a rupee (only).

11. Diwali comes once a year (only).

12. I have thought of marrying (often).

13. We eat two meals a day (only).

14. Your boots want mending (badly).

15. I am anxious to see him (only).

16. I met him once (only).

17. The chair cost Rs 150 (only).

18. He has slept two hours (only).

19. He wrote on one side of the paper (only).

44

Correct Use of Prepositions

The following prepositions require careful notice:

(1) We use *in* with cities, towns and villages when we think of them as areas. We use *at* when we see the city, town or village as a point on a journey.

We stayed in London for three days.

Our plane stopped at London on the way to New York.

I have lived in this village for five years.

Does the bus stop at that village ?

(2) We use *at* to talk about addresses. If we merely give the name of the street, we use *in*.

They live *at* 72 Tilak Street.

They live *in* Tilak Street.

(3) We use *in* with parts of the day.

I will see him *in* the afternoon/ *in* the evening.

Exception : *at* night

We say *on* + a day + a part of the day.

I will see him *on* Saturday afternoon.

(4) Note the use of *since* and *for* in the perfect tenses. *Since* is used with a point of time and *for* with a period of time.

since	8 o'clock last week 2nd May 2001 my childhood	*for*	two hours several days a fortnight three years a long time

I have known him { *since* 2000
{ *for* a long time.

We have been waiting { *since* 9.30.
{ *for* an hour.

(5) *Till* is used of *time,* and *to* is used of *place;* as,
    I slept *till* eight o'clock.

They waited *till* sunset.

They fasted *till* the hour of prayer.

They wept *till* dawn.

They stopped *till* the end of the day.

He walked *to* the end of the road.

(6) *With* often denotes the *instrument,* and *by* the *agent;* as,

He killed two birds *with* one shot.

He was stabbed *by* a lunatic.

(7) *In* before a noun denoting a period of time, means *at the end of;* *within* means *before the end of;* as,

I shall return *in* an hour.

I shall return *within* an hour.

EXERCISE 1

Insert the right *Preposition* in each of the following sentences:

1. The dog jumped .... the river (in, into).
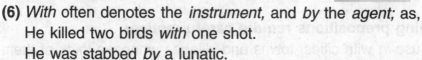

2. The portrait was painted .... a famous artist (with, by).

3. I have not seen him .... a long time (for, since).

4. He was killed .... the robber .... a hatchet (by, with).

5. How long have you stayed ..... this village ? (in, at)

6. We live ..... 36 Park Street. (in, at)

7. He has been working in this factory .... three years. (since, for)

8. She has been ill ...... last month. (since, for)

9. We met him ..... Sunday morning. (on, in)

10. We walked from the museum .... the station. (till, to)

EXERCISE 2

Fill up the blanks with appropriate *Prepositions*:

1. He has spent his life .... Delhi.

2. I saw him felling a big tree .... a hatchet.

3. He travelled 120 km .... two hours.

4. He is laid down with fever .... yesterday.

5. He rushed .... my room, panting for breath.

6. The Rajdhani Express is due .... 3 p.m.

7. The child has been missing .... last Tuesday.

8. The portrait was painted .... Ravi Verma.

9. He hanged himself .... a piece of cloth.

10. He was born .... a small village .... Gujarat.

The preposition is usually placed *before* the noun or pronoun it governs, but it is often placed at the *end* of the sentence when the relative pronoun is omitted; as,

That is the boy (*whom*) I was speaking *of.*

In interrogative sentences the preposition is often placed at the end; as,

What are you talking *about* ?

What is this made *of* ?

What do you want me *for* ?

Who are you looking *for* ?

When the object is the relative pronoun *that,* the preposition is always placed at the end; as,

Here is the book *that* you asked *for.*

This is the boy *that* I spoke *of.*

The preposition is also placed at the end when emphasis is required; as,

This I insist *on.*

Such *conduct* I am at a loss to account *for.*

Certain verbs, nouns, and adjectives are always followed by particular Prepositions. Read the following sentences, noting the correct preposition after each word in italics.

He *agreed to* my proposal.

He *supplied* the poor *with* clothing.

Silk-worms *feed on* mulberry leaves.

He is *engaged to* my cousin.

He was *punished for* misconduct.

She was *dressed in* a white saree.

I beg leave to *differ from* you.

I *warned* him *of* the danger.

We should *provide against* risk of fire by insuring our goods.

The goat *subsists on* the coarsest of food.

He was *born of* poor parents.

Beware of pickpockets.

The doctor *cured* him *of* asthma.

What is the *matter with* the child ?

I had *difficulty in* finding his address.

Little Jack proved quite a *match for* the giant.

This drug acts as a *preventive of* malaria.

He is *dependent on* his parents.

He is *bound by* a contract.

He is *deficient in* common sense.

He is *indifferent to* his own interest.

He is *blind of* one eye.

The Moors were *famous for* their learning.

Oil is *good for* burns.

Alcohol is *injurious to* health.

This pencil is *different from* that.

He is *related to* me.

He is *ill with* fever.

EXERCISE 3

Supply correct *Prepositions* to fill the blanks:

1. A wise man profits .... experience.
2. I have a picture similar .... yours.
3. You may rely .... what he says.
4. He has no taste .... music.
5. You will be sorry .... your mistake.
6. His face is familiar .... me.
7. His sister died .... consumption.
8. He is married .... my cousin.
9. The jury found him guilty .... murder.

10. Take care .... your health.
11. My sister is fond .... fairy tales.
12. The dog is faithful .... his master.
13. This house is suitable .... a large family.
14. He is always in need .... money.
15. He is acquainted .... all the facts.
16. She is fond .... children.
17. Never yield .... temptations.
18. His face reminds me .... his father.
19. This rose differs .... that.
20. He is very different .... what I expected.

21. The ship is infested .... rats.

22. I cannot agree .... your proposal.

23. The Kangaroo is an animal peculiar .... Australia.

24. Wisdom is often compared .... gold.

25. I prefer coffee .... tea.

26. He was born .... Kolkata .... humble parents.

27. We should be thankful .... God .... all His gifts.

28. The room is full .... people.

29. I deeply sympathize .... you.

30. He was warned .... the danger.

EXERCISE 4

Supply correct *Prepositions* to fill the blanks:

1. You must watch .... an opportunity.

2. The old woman is weary .... life.

3. Attend .... your work.

4. I will comply .... your request.

5. Allow me to remind you .... your promise.

6. I must inquire .... the matter.

7. I congratulate you .... your success.

8. I beg to differ .... you.

9. He has recovered .... his illness.

10. The artist takes a pride .... his work.

11. Be on your guard .... burglars.

12. I am going to compete .... the prize.

13. He has lost the use .... his right arm.

14. The stories in that book are full .... interest.

15. He proved false .... his friend.

16. He is not ashamed .... his conduct.

17. We should rely .... our own efforts.

18. He insisted .... going.

19. He could not give a satisfactory explanation .... his absence.

It is a hard task!

20. My brother is weak .... arithmetic.

21. I am sick .... the whole business.

22. You have hardly any chance .... succeeding.

23. I am obliged .... you .... your kindness.

24. I am tired .... writing letters to him.

Chapter 45

Subject and Predicate
(Revise Chapter 1)

We have learnt that every sentence that we speak or write consists of two parts, the Subject and the Predicate.

The person or thing about which something is said, is called the **Subject.**

What is said about the Subject is called the **Predicate.**

SUBJECT	PREDICATE
Birds	fly.
Cows	eat grass.
That horse	is white.
A cold wind	blew last night.
The boy	stood on the burning deck.
The little lamb	followed Mary everywhere.
To read good books	is delightful.
[You*]	Sit down.

* *You* is here understood. It is therefore enclosed in brackets.

Examine these sentences :

1. Mary had a little lamb.
2. Little Hari is the cleverest boy in the class.
3. The poor old woman gets little food.

Which is the Subject in sentence 1 ? — *Mary.*

Which is the Subject in sentence 2 ? — *Little Hari.*

Here the Subject consists of more than one word. Which is the most important word in the Subject ? The noun *Hari* is clearly the most important word in the Subject : without it we cannot form the Subject. We call it therefore the **Subject-word** or the **Simple Subject** to distinguish it from the Complete Subject.

Which is the Subject in sentence 3 ? — *The poor old woman.*

Here the noun *woman* is the most important word in the Subject. Therefore the noun *woman* is the Subject-word or the Simple Subject.

We now divide or analyse the above sentences, italicising the Simple Subject:

No.	SUBJECT	PREDICATE
1.	Mary	had a little lamb.
2.	Little *Hari*	is the cleverest boy in the class.
3.	The poor old *woman*	gets little food.

EXERCISE

Divide the following sentences into Subject and Predicate, and underline the *Subject Word*:

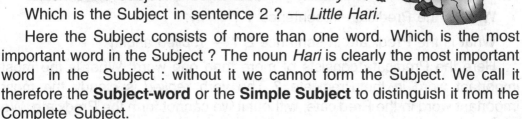

1. The foolish crow tried to sing.
2. Bad boys hide their faults.
3. My new watch keeps good time.
4. The hungry child wept bitterly.
5. Little Bo-peep has lost her sheep.
6. A cold wind blew last night.
7. Your book lies on the desk.
8. Old Tubal Cain was a man of might.
9. Small people love to talk of great.
10. The morning sun shall dawn again.
11. The little lamb followed Mary everywhere.
12. The old woman looks unhappy.

Examine these sentences :

1. Birds fly.
2. The boss replied angrily.
3. She writes her copybook neatly.

What is the Predicate in sentence 1 ? — *fly.*

What is the Predicate in sentence 2 ? — *replied angrily.*

Here the Predicate consists of more than one word. What is the most important word in the Predicate ? The verb *replied* is clearly the most important word in the Predicate: without it we cannot form the Predicate. We call it the **Simple Predicate** or the **Predicate-Verb** to distinguish it from the Complete Predicate.

What is the Predicate in sentence 3 ? –- *writes her copybook neatly.* What is the most important word in the Predicate ? The verb *writes.*

It will be noticed that every Predicate is either a Verb or contains a Verb, because no Predicate can be formed without a Verb.

We now break up or analyse the above sentences, putting the Verb in a separate column.

No.	SUBJECT	PREDICATE	
		Verb	*Rest of Predicate*
1.	Birds	fly.	
2.	The boss	replied	angrily.
3.	She	writes	her copybook neatly.

It will be noticed that in sentence 1 the Predicate is simply a Verb.

Examine these sentences :

1. Bad boys hide their faults.
2. Shirin's mother is ill.
3. The village master taught his little school.

Which is the Complete Subject in sentence 1 ? — *Bad boys.*

Which is the Subject-word ? The noun *boys.*

The word *bad* which goes with the Subject-word *boys* is called in Analysis the **Enlargement of the Subject**.

Which is the Complete Subject in sentence 2 ? *Shirin's mother.*

Which is the Subject-word ? — *mother.* The word *Shirin's which goes with the Subject-word is the Enlargement of the Subject.*

Which words go with the Subject-word in sentence 3 ?

Now examine how we break up or analyse the above sentences.

No.	SUBJECT		PREDICATE	
	Subject-word.	*Enlargement of Subject.*	*Verb*	*Rest of Predicate*
1.	boys	Bad	hide	their faults.
2.	mother	Shirin's	is	ill.
3.	master	(1) The (2) village	taught	his little school.

49

Extension of the Predicate

Examine these sentences :

1. The boss replied angrily.
2. She writes her copybook neatly.
3. You have done your lesson well.

Which is the Predicate in sentence 1 ? — *replied angrily.*

Which is the Verb in this Predicate ? — *replied.*

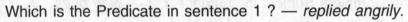

The Adverb *angrily* which goes with the verb *replied* is called in Analysis the **Extension of the Predicate**.

Which is the Predicate in sentence 2 ? — *writes her copybook neatly.*

Which is the Verb in this Predicate ? — *writes.*

The Adverb *neatly* goes with the verb *writes.* It is therefore the Extension of the Predicate.

Which is the Extension of the Predicate in sentence 3?

Now carefully examine how we break up or analyse the above sentences.

No.	SUBJECT		PREDICATE		
	Subject-word	*Enlargement of Subject*	*Verb*	*Extension Predicate*	*Rest of Predicate*
1.	boss	The	replied	angrily	
2.	She		writes	neatly	her copybook
3.	You		have done	well	your lesson

It will be noticed that we now make a separate column for the Extension of the Predicate.

EXERCISE

Analyse the following sentences :

1. Hari runs swiftly.

2. The girl sings beautifully.

3. The servants are paid monthly.

4. I know him well.

5. He has come back.

6. I shall return soon.

7. The hungry child wept bitterly.

8. My uncle lives there.

9. The little lamb followed Mary everywhere.

10. He hit the ball hard.

11. He spends his money foolishly.

Examine these sentences :

1. She writes her copybook neatly.
2. You have done your lesson well.
3. A barking sound the shepherd hears.

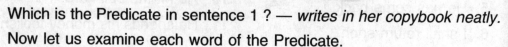

Which is the Predicate in sentence 1 ? — *writes in her copybook neatly.*

Now let us examine each word of the Predicate.

writes	Verb
neatly	Extension of Predicate
copybook	Object

The word *her* which goes with the Object *copybook* is called in Analysis the **Enlargement of the Object**.

In sentence 2 the word *your* which goes with the Object *lesson* is the Enlargement of the Object.

Which is the Object in sentence 3 ? Which words go with the Object ?

Now examine how we break up or analyse these sentences.

SUBJECT		PREDICATE			
Subject-word	Enlargement of Subject	Verb	Object	Enlargement of Object	Extension of Predicate
She		writes	copy-book	her	neatly
You		have done	lesson	your	well
shepherd	the	hears	sound	(1) A (2) barking	

EXERCISE

Analyse **the following sentences :**

1. The cow loves her calf.
2. Children should obey their parents.
3. The spider has eight legs.
4. The hungry child wept bitterly.
5. I badly want some money.

6. The boy made the kite cleverly.
7. The children found a bird's nest.
8. Aladdin had a wonderful lamp.
9. Somebody has just stolen my new watch.
10. I met a little cottage girl.

When I say 'The baby laughs,' you understand what I mean. The sentence makes complete sense.

But when I say 'The baby is,' you want to know *what* the baby is. The group of words 'The baby is' does not make complete sense. Why ? Because the verb 'is' does not make good sense alone; it requires a word after it (such as the word 'happy') to complete its meaning.

Such as the verb 'is,' which does not make good sense alone, is called an **Incomplete Verb** or **Verb of Incomplete Predication**, and the word 'happy' which *completes* its meaning is called its **Complement**.

The following sentences contain some other Incomplete Verbs. Notice that the complement is a Noun, or an Adjective, or a Pronoun.

He appears a *rogue.* Peel became *minister.*
Rama became *sad.*   The sky grew *dark.*
She seems *unhappy.* He looked *pale.*
It is *him.*

When you analyse a sentence containing a Verb of Incomplete Predication, put the **Complement** in a separate column.

SUBJECT	PREDICATE	
	Verb	*Complement*
Ram Singh	is	a soldier
He	became	angry

EXERCISE

Pick out the *Verb* and the *Complement* in each of the following sentences :

1. The rumour seems true.
2. The nights became cold.
3. The child fell asleep.
4. At last the sea became calm.
5. The mangoes taste delicious.
6. One of the eleven fell ill.
7. The old woman looks unhappy.
8. The poor coolie seems tired.
9. The wind is cold.
10. The report proved false.
11. The poor woman went mad.
12. The boys made a noise.

Chapter 52

Analysis of Simple Sentences

Examine how the following sentences are analysed :

1. My little brother has learnt to read.
2. She gave him food.
3. I am going home.
4. Where shall we go ?
5. The jury found him guilty.

SUBJECT		PREDICATE			
Subject-word	*Enlargement of Subject*	*Verb*	*Object*	*Complement*	*Extension of Predicate*
brother	(1) My (2) little	has learnt	to read		
She		gave	(1) him (2) food		
I		am going			home
We		shall go			Where
jury	The	found	him	guilty	

It will be noticed that in sentence 2 the verb has *two* objects.

EXERCISE 1

Analyse the following sentences :

1. The boy made the kite cleverly.
2. The children found a bird's nest.
3. The poor old man seems tired.

4. My new gold watch keeps good time.
5. Do not talk such nonsense.
6. The post has already come today.

7. I have walked miles.

8. Many lay dead.

9. The dog followed the girl patiently everywhere.

10. We taught the dog tricks.

11. The boys elected him captain.

12. Call the man back.

Examine the following sentences :

1. Gardens with cool shady trees surround the village.

   [*What* gardens ? — *with cool shady trees.*]

2. Houses built of stone are strong.

   [*What* houses ? — *built of stone.*]

3. Permission to play games was granted.

   [*What sort of* permission ? — *to play games.*]

It will be noticed that, in each of the above sentences, the Enlargement of the Subject is a *group* of words.

Now, examine this sentence :

Wild beasts in small cages are a sorry sight.

Here there are two Enlargements of the Subject:

(1) Wild, (2) in small cages.

EXERCISE 2

Pick out the *Enlargements* of the *Subject* in the following sentences:

1. The book on the desk is mine.

2. The lion in that cage is old.

3. A book in big type is easy to read.

4. The mangoes in that basket are ripe.

5. The house by the river is for sale.

6. The man of wealth should help the poor.

7. The tops of the mountains were covered with snow.

8. The crowd in the bazaar was very noisy.

9. All the shops in the market were closed yesterday.

10. Fearing to be caught in the rain, we returned.

11. Driven by hunger, he stole a piece of bread.

12. Walking along a road, a boy found a watch.

13. An attempt to kill the king was unsuccessful.

14. The story, told by the prisoner, may be true.

15. Unconscious of the danger he slept.

It will be noticed that in each of the following sentences, the Enlargement of the Object is a *group* of words:

1. The Eskimos make houses *of snow and ice.*
2. I met him *coming down the street.*
3. I saw cords *stretched across the road.*

Now examine this sentence :

Have you seen the man in the moon ?

Here there are two Enlargements of the Object : (1) the, (2) in the moon.

EXERCISE 3

Pick out the *Enlargements* of the *Object* in the following sentences:

1. The children have read the story of Ali Baba.
2. Have you seen a rose without thorn ?
3. I saw a boy eating figs.
4. Soldiers guarded the entrance of the castle.
5. Once I saw a man with a wooden leg.
6. I shall buy that bunch of flowers.
7. He wore a turban of red silk.
8. We reached a path covered with mud.

9. Nobody likes a person with a bad temper.
10. The architect drew a plan for the house.
11. In a low voice he told the tale of his cruel wrongs.
12. I had no answer to my letter.
13. I have forgotten the name of the author.
14. The Rajah has a writing-desk made of ivory.
15. We saw a man leading a monkey.
16. He bore a banner with a strange device.

Examine the following sentences :

1. He ran with all his might.

   [Ran *how* ? — *with all his might.*]
2. He ran down the street.

   [Ran *where* ? — *down the street.*]
3. He ran to catch a thief.

   [Ran *why* ? — *to catch a thief.*]
4. He returned after an hour.

   [Returned *when* ? — *after an hour.*]

It will be noticed that, in each of the above sentences, the Extension of the Predicate consists of a *group* of words.

EXERCISE 4

Pick out the *Extension* **of the** *Predicate* **in each of the following sentences :**

1. She spoke in a whisper.
2. The farmer's wife jumped out of bed.
3. The train is going at full speed.
4. The picture hangs on the wall.
5. The boy stood on the burning deck.
6. He acted against my advice.
7. The man rode on a white horse.
8. He cut his finger with a penknife.
9. The tide having turned, the ship set sail.
10. With my bow and arrow I killed Cock Robin.
11. Under a spreading chestnut tree the village smithy stands.
12. The sun having risen, we started.
13. I left my luggage at the station.
14. A mouse awakened a lion from sleep.
15. We shall learn to write in a year.

We now analyse the last three sentences.

SUBJECT		PREDICATE			
Subject-word	Enlargement of Subject	Verb	Object	Enlargement of Object	Extension of Predicate
I		left	luggage	my	at the station
mouse	A	awaken-ed	lion	a	from sleep
We		shall learn	to write		in a year